PRESERVATION

PRESERVATION

Peter Svenson

Faber and Faber
BOSTON • LONDON

Copyright © 1994 by Peter Svenson

Library of Congress Cataloging-in-Publication Data

Svenson, Peter.
    Preservation / Peter Svenson.
        p. cm.
    ISBN 0-571-19840-6
    1. Historic preservation—United States.   2. United States—
History—Civil War, 1861–1865—Battlefields.   3. Historic sites—
United States—Conservation and restoration.   4. Svenson, Peter—
Homes and haunts—Virginia—Cross Keys.   I. Title.
E159.S84   1994
363.6'9'0973—dc20   93-42835
                                                                                                            CIP

Jacket design by Adrian Morgan at Red Letter Design
Jacket photograph courtesy of Photonica

Printed in the United States of America

for Mr. Palmer and Mrs. Trefethen

ἄγροικόσ εἰμι τήν σκάφην σκάφην λέγω.
"I'm a rustic; the tub's a tub, I say."

Often translated as

"I'm from the country; I call a spade a spade."
–*comic Attic fragment*

Loss of innocence, loss of fortune, loss of war, loss of a leader or a lover or a friend . . . There exists a well-rounded—and well-received—body of literature concerning human loss, for it is a subject that quantifies maturity and is, ultimately, the best preparation for our own dissolution.

But what of preservation? What do we keep and why do we keep it? Is there not another kind of maturity in the maintenance of things, in the continuation of an original impulse in a way that accomplishes a different preparation—a redirection toward the beginning instead of the end? This is what I've been pondering recently.

Cross Keys, Virginia
October 1993

PRESERVATION

ONE

ONE OF THE BENEFITS of living at the center of a rural Civil War battlefield is the privilege of sitting down at the piano and banging out "Dixie" and "The Battle Hymn of the Republic" whenever I feel like it.

The mood descends upon me often enough. My home on the once-bloodied ground at Cross Keys, in Rockingham County in Virginia's Shenandoah Valley, is ideally suited for flights of acoustic fancy. In my studio at the edge of forty acres of hayfield, I can bang out pretty much any tune I want, or sing at the top of my lungs. My family is lovingly inured to "Dad doing his thing," and the nearest neighbor who might object to my musical eruptions is half a mile away.

During a typical hour of piano practice, my fingers seek out the two Civil War marches, back to back, as either a warm-up or a wrap-up. Both tunes stand out from the run-of-the-mill contemporary repertoire I habitually fine-tune and sporadically perform. My piano jobs, when I have them, occur in upscale lounges, or at mall fashion shows, or at wedding receptions. I stock my song list with the mellowed chestnuts that perennially bob up on the airwaves. Love and nostalgia in every imaginable aspect are what people want to hear, and consequently what I purvey. "Dixie" and "The Battle Hymn" are different (as well as being different from each other) because they are embodiments of collective hope, antidotes to national despair. And they are over 130 years old. Although the two marches galvanized America's nineteenth-century population enmeshed in civil strife, today they are stirring anomalies beached by the fickle tides of contemporary taste. Alongside the newest of the new wave, the old songs are unavoidably quaint. In my lifetime, only a march like "The Yellow Rose of Texas" has captured the American public's attention to such a degree, although for a while during the

1960s Bob Dylan's "Rainy Day Woman #12 & 35" (with its refrain, "Everybody must get stoned") may have run a close second.

The words and melody to "Dixie"—also entitled "Dixieland," "(I Wish I Was In) Dixie," or "Dixie's Land"—were written for the music-hall venue by Dan Emmett,[1] an Ohioan, and published in 1860. As the march gained in popularity, it became emblematic of the Rebel Cause. Meanwhile, Julia Ward Howe's poem "Battle Hymn" first appeared in *The Atlantic Monthly* in 1861. William Steffe, a Southerner, had written a camp meeting hymn in Charleston, South Carolina, in 1852 called "Say, Brother, Will We Meet You Over on the Other Shore?" By 1862, Ward's lyric and Steffe's music were wedded in the unforgettable clarion that became a favorite with the marching bands of the Union Army. Often called simply "Glory, Hallelujah," the march proclaimed the moral high ground of the anti-slavery, pro-Union forces, and predicted the coming victory. A variant was known as "John Brown's Body."

When I play the two marches on the piano, I experience feelings that transcend the mere joy of a workout for my fingers. In the music of the marches—the one with a lilting catchiness, the other with a swaggering exultancy—I perceive a glimmer of the American consciousness of the 1860s. "Dixie," that secular passion-rouser, energizes me like a collegiate fight song, while "The Battle Hymn" summons the fervidness of a religious testimonial. In the lyrics of both marches, the first person point of view elicits strong identification: "Mine eyes have seen the glory . . ." and ". . . In Dixieland, I'll take my stand." Indeed, the two tunes strike me as masterworks of persuasion. As I play them, I am momentarily transported back to the partisanship of the Civil War. Like two sides of a coin, each complementing the other, the marches belong together. I never play one without playing the other. I always start with "Dixie," as if I, too, were a partner in the hurly-burly breakout of secessionism, just as I follow—scarcely missing a beat—with "The Battle Hymn," falling in step with the inevitable rectitude of a reunited nation.

This private and seemingly inconsequential behavior on my part has profound implications, I am convinced. What I am doing is preserving the emotional heritage of the American Civil War. If I were only hearing the marches on the radio and identifying them—a test, I suspect, numerous citizens might fail nowadays—I would not be doing enough. I am seeking a deeper understanding, and consequently a deeper gratification.

---

[1] Recent research shows that Emmett may have learned the song from the Snowden family, African-American musicians in his hometown of Mount Vernon, Ohio.

Too often I've been just a listener soothed by a steady stream of banalities ("And now we bring you an uninterrupted half hour of your favorites—only on WJAM!"). If I were living on the battlefield and had accomplished nothing else by way of its preservation, just the fact that I whistled or hummed "Dixie" and "The Battle Hymn" would exonerate me to a certain degree, because it would show that I was constructively employed in the work of remembrance. It would show that I was not afraid to reach back into the past. And if I were a different person, more politically and regionally aligned, I might hum one march and not the other, and that would be okay, too, because it would show that I harbored strong feelings, one way or the other.

But living here for eight years and coming to grips with the history of the land, and, moreover, farming the land, I am beyond the point of partisan preference. Practicing the piano is the least of my activities; it is the vestige of a childhood duty, one that became a labor of love and now has the added dimension of habit. If I go more than a few days without an honest hour of practice, I feel terrible about myself. In my mind, I have preserved the admonitions of my childhood piano teacher, a taskmistress if there ever was one, who coaxed the nearest thing to perfection from her students. Her own professional life had been woefully imperfect. After I left her tutelage, I learned that she had been an eminently promising Julliard graduate who abandoned plans for a concert career when she realized that her stage fright was unmanageable. It took me twenty years to appreciate the gift she gave me. With her help, I developed an artistic talent. It wasn't my gift, it was *her* gift. And although my talent has never approached the rarefied art of a concert pianist, it has been serviceable enough to keep me employed part-time at various stages of my life as a keyboard player in a band, and most recently as an occasional soloist.

So I sit at my venerable Mason & Hamlin and rip through "Dixie" and "The Battle Hymn." I am preserving the emotional pitch of the Civil War. I am also preserving my training as a skinny kid on a creaking piano bench—a hater of weekly lessons and a shirker of daily practice, but nevertheless, a music maker.

Preservation. The specimen under the bell jar, the contents of a can. Preservation is a word that conjures up collections in a natural history museum: beady-eyed birds gripping desiccated twigs, molting foxes frozen at a trot on cotton snow. It is a word that is fraught with wax and glass and acid-free paper, vitrines with watered silk interiors, hushed lighting. It is the conservator's painstaking skill at the removal of varnish and soot. It is the presence of uniformed guards standing (or sitting on a stool) hour after watchful hour until closing time. It is the rallying cry of the landmark-conscious, who embark on rescue missions of inanimate objects: buildings, neighborhoods, battlefields. And in its largest sense, preservation is the wrapping of the planet in the duct tape of love. Things have gotten that far out of hand.

Two years shy of the half-century mark, I empathize intensely with all of the above, but I find myself focusing on matters closer to home, nearer to the heart. It is the person within me that needs preserving. If I don't do something about it now, I may veer off on a tangent of comfort and conformity, losing sight of the person I was before I became the person I am. In middle age I think of myself as a bulging file of experience, something lavishly and affectionately added to over the years, something that was originally slender and will eventually need to be pared down.

So I've decided to open the drawer and do a little selective sorting out. Present and past have been stuffed willy-nilly. No proponent of linear order, I have lived my life in a fluid way, overlapping and interweaving as events shaped me. To perform this act of preservation of self and surroundings, I'll need a modicum of discipline, the confines of these pages for starters, and an agenda that will allow me to cut and paste as I see fit.

I am just old enough to reflect on my accomplishments and failures with a jaundiced eye. I would sooner forget everything I've gone through than go through it again. Growing up has been a trying experience. The adult child is at a dangerous age, especially when the realization kicks in that growing up is never over. That encompassing term, "middle age," is a frightening three syllables, a stalled plateau from which to say, "Whew!" to the past and "Wow!" to the future. One false step, and I'm plunged into the canyon. Can you believe it, I'm more than halfway down the countdown? In the mirror, the lines on my face startle me into the starting blocks of new races. Life gets more complicated. I compete against my younger self. In the course of a day, my self-appointed list of tasks grows like Pinocchio's nose. I lie to myself that I will get them all done; I'm lucky if I finish one.

Until I came to the battlefield, I was anchorless, even though I had dropped anchor numerous times. Perhaps there's a better way to put it: my hawser was severed repeatedly. Before I built our house here, I had built three others, each on rural acreage, each with studio space so that I could pursue my true, though frequently interrupted vocation as an artist. Each immersion in house-building was a laying of the groundwork, so to speak, for posterity. With each ambitious project, I was setting myself up for a quiet life in the country, for intense and remunerative production in the studio, for a harmonious familial surround.

Although I set my sights on a career in visual art, in abstract painting, I did not rule out other aspects of the continuum of creativity, ones for which I knew I had a demonstrated flair. I tried my hand at prose. I tried my hand at poetry. I played and sang folk guitar, and spent a number of years training myself to be a songwriter. And all the while I held a succession of odd jobs: a hired helper, an electrician, a college instructor, a farm worker, a furniture salesperson, and so forth. Last but not least, I was a househusband and a full time father.

I found that the creative trying (and it was steady and serious pursuit, not dilettantish) undermined the stability of everything else I was bent on accomplishing. It was next to impossible to make both art and a living. I grew to resent the interruptions, but more to the point, I grew to resent my lack of artistic success. The lucky breaks that seemed just around the corner were mirages. The curly-headed iconoclast became the balding tilter at windmills. Recognition and its attendant rewards seemed to recede like my hairline, and there was nothing in my power to reverse the process. I kept trying—changing, switching, revamping, reassessing. A bigger and better *something* was needed. A truer, purer *somehow*.

An early marriage curdled after a difficult decade. I threw myself into a fit of creativity. I could lose my wife, lose my house, lose custody of my children, lose my self-constructed bulwark against everything that antagonized and demoralized me, but I could not lose my artistic vision. A painting I did at the time, entitled *The Happy Man*, illustrated the intensity of my grip as I clung to this intangible. Abstractly, the painting is a self-portrait of me dancing in front of my house—something I've never actually done, nor even consciously thought of doing. A bitter and defiant picture (and a tad garish, as I see it in retrospect), it sums up the way I was feeling. In my emptiness, there was nothing left to bother with, or to be bothered by. I could kick up my heels and prance as if gravity itself had been knocked out from under me.

To maintain my *raison d'être* as an artist, I tried hard to expand my credibility within the art world, but at this low point, not a single gallery that had exhibited my work in the past would give me a show. The pendulum swing of popularity was moving away from the kind of painting I did. I kept hammering away at the major metropolitan markets by sending slide sheets in the mail with return postage, but nothing came

of my efforts. Nearer exhibition venues were closed off to me as well—
the foyers of banks, the walls of restaurants. Edged out locally by the
regionalist's genre (dappled byways, foals in pasture, lissome women in
straw hats) and edged out in the cities by the monumental put-ons and
puns of the svelte tyros dressed in black, my work was denied access to
the viewing public.

I settled for the next best thing: art consignment. A few scattered
galleries were willing to "give me a try" by accepting a canvas or two on
a consignment basis. For these crumbs I was genuinely grateful. I drove
many hundreds of miles, delivering paintings wherever the scant havens
were made available. Hopeful, ever so hopeful, I played the waiting
game, waiting for my work to be "discovered," an eventuality that got
remoter as month after futile month rolled by. Once or twice in a blue
moon I'd get lucky and find a modest check in the mail. Mostly, though,
my paintings were tucked away in the racks and bins, and when
sufficient exposure time had passed without so much as a nibble, I'd receive a curt note demanding that I please pick up the work, as it was
taking up much-needed space. Dutifully, I'd hit the road. Sometimes I'd
be able to talk a gallery director into exchanging old work for new, but
more often than not, I drove home with the added cargo. Lugging my
shopworn canvases back inside the empty house—empty, that is, except
for the burgeoning oeuvre that remained unsold—I'd feel the loss of
familial fullness and wonder why I had ever embarked on such a
crooked, rewardless path. As an artist, I was getting nowhere.

I moved fifty miles across the mountains to the Shenandoah Valley
to live with an old friend from graduate school who had been handed
her walking papers the same time I had been handed mine. Two ten-year
marriages, two devastating breakups—a symmetry that set the stage for
our falling in love. We got over the hurt together, and she remains to
this day the sweetest miracle that ever happened in my life.

When Becky and I were married, we were living in her small brick
house in Harrisonburg with its claw-footed bathtub and an unfinished
quilt for a bathroom door. The remnants of our former households,
now combined, were spilling out from every corner. Our artwork—
Becky is an artist, too, in addition to being an art professor—was stacked
against the walls. Boxfuls of belongings narrowed the passageways. The
dining-room table doubled as a makeshift studio. On weekends and
school vacations when my children, Hope and Van, were with us, our
living quarters shrank even more; we had become a family starved for
floor space.

To forestall the approaching critical mass, we bought a fourteen-acre Christmas tree farm six miles out of town on the brow of a hill overlooking the farming community of Cross Keys. There I intended to build a spacious, studio-winged two-story house, but before I began I had to tear down a derelict farmhouse on the site as well as its outbuildings, then clean up the lingering trash of several environmentally unmindful generations. Following this, the limestone shelf had to be blasted and re-shaped to accommodate the new foundation. My year-long effort resulted in a good house, not a great house, but the pleasure of living in it was cut short when our nearest neighbor erected a poultry barn longer than three football fields against our common boundary. I had just harvested two hundred Christmas trees (and planted two thousand more) when it dawned on me that my tree-farming career was cancelled. Nobody in his or her right mind would go through what I had gone through just to be a sensory prisoner in the foul shadow of agribusiness.

Selling the tree farm, we bought forty acres of pasture-land and hay-field on the plain at Cross Keys, which turned out to have been the epicenter of the Civil War battle. I built another house. I began hay farming. I wrote a book.

And now I am sitting at the piano, bounding along the steeplechase of "Dixie" and navigating the estuary of "The Battle Hymn." I have come through the normal development span of one career with four: farming, painting, writing, piano-playing. All along, I've been hedging my bets — winning on a good hand, losing on a bad one, but staying in the game. If there is a mist before my eyes, it is not the mist of sentimentality but rather the opacity of remembrance. Like anyone else, I tend to forget the past — mine, my nation's, my civilization's — because I am too caught up in the present *per se*. I have honed myself to be a student of the contemporary scene, a firm-footed dweller in and observer of the here and now, but when I get too hung up on the moment, I am not always capable of my clearest and most sensitive thinking. The present resonates with its full meaning only when the past is right behind it like the skeleton beneath the skin. Fortunately for me, the landscape I live in is irregular with the juttings of history. Daily, I am reminded of the need to work on this business of preservation.

TWO

A VERY SHORT GRANITE OBELISK (vaguely proportionate to a dog house) sits atop a limestone cube that rests at the center of a flagstone square about ten feet on a side ringed by an iron picket fence. This is the monument commemorating the place where Confederate Brigadier General Turner Ashby died on June 6, 1862. It is located at the edge of an oak grove, hard against a pair of concrete pylons that bear a high voltage transmission line, at the end of a quiet lane just inside the city limits of Harrisonburg. Cavalry commander in Stonewall Jackson's army and holder of a reputation for dashing bravery, Ashby was a folk hero whose untimely death in a skirmish occasioned great shock and sorrow among his fellow Virginians.

The monument was erected in 1898, thirty-three years after the close of the Civil War, by a group of townspeople and veterans who called themselves the Turner Ashby Memorial Association. The veracity of the monument's location as being the actual spot where Ashby fell has never been ascertained, but it is in the general vicinity. Port Republic Road, a busy artery heading southeast of town, passes through the skirmish ground. The lane leading to the monument is less than half a mile long. It was paved for the first time in 1992.

The gravel lane, as I had known it for years, ran between several back-yards and a pasture or two before it terminated in leafy woods that were gradually being appropriated for building lots. Prior to paving, it was widened and re-graded; now, ebonized with asphalt, the lane sits high between ditches, transecting the terrain as it never did before. Parallel to it, the electric transmission line is strung on gray pylons, zigging to the right at the monument, zagging to the left a couple hundred feet later, then disappearing over the crest of the wooded hill. Beneath this right of way, a brown herbicide-controlled strip numbs the fields, giving the appearance of a six o'clock shadow. In the distance are clusters of taupe-walled apartments. These are the environs of the outer reaches of the city limits. Not rural anymore, but not overly developed either, it is a limbo that will retain an existential emptiness for decades, delineated by other utility right of ways, housing starts, empty lots for sale.

The former pastureland is eroding at an alarming rate, but nobody is alarmed. Red clay clogs the gullies and lies exposed on inclines where ragweed and broomsedge are no match for the pounding of rain. A concrete sewer abutment is emplaced, yet isolated like a kiln or a bomb shelter. Neither fish nor fowl, the land is clearly slated for development *at some future date*, but today it is marking time, obscured in the nimbus of a faltering economy.

On these empty slopes where nothing is going on save the hum of electrical energy along the overhead wires, Turner Ashby made his last stand. He was a fatalistic fighter and bon vivant who seriously believed that the Yankees could do him no harm. His horse was shot from under him; dismounted, he took a few sword-brandishing steps before he, too, was felled by a bullet. Not far away, beside the highway in the condos that bear his name, James Madison University students are studying at formica work stations, or sunbathing beside the chlorinated rectangle of blue. Late sleepers, fledgling lovers lie abed. In the parking lots, Hondas, Hyundais, Izuzus, Mitsubishis, Nissans, Subarus, and Toyotas glow like scarabs, berthed between parallel painted lines. The little cars and pickup trucks are asleep, too, like docile, indolent toys that will purr (or roar) with joy when they are awakened. And around and between the apartments and parking lots are tall, tapering aluminum poles that support mercury vapor lamps. These are the landscapers' true marks, not the anemic bushes that straddle patches of pine bark mulch, nor the dying flowers that bend their heads toward the curbs.

In 1991, during a lull in civic affairs, an editor of the local newspaper decided that a proposal to pave the gravel lane that led to the Ashby monument would make good copy. In trenchant journalese, the lane was depicted as a bumpy and dusty eyesore that offended visitors from out of town and diminished the memory of the great General Ashby because it was not in keeping with the fine road system already established within the city limits, et cetera. To strengthen his argument, the editor took it upon himself to upgrade Ashby's final skirmish—or rearguard action, to put it more precisely—into a full-scale battle: the Battle of Harrisonburg. *Now* it was something to crow about. For the benefit of the ignorant public, the misnomer was fleshed out in stirring detail: the apocryphal eyewitness descriptions of valor, the bogus certitude of where and when and how many, the last words attributable to the dying man. A coda to the article included the genesis of a penny-ante trust, the Turner Ashby Fund, which would collect the six thousand dollars necessary to hire a paving contractor (at a cut rate) to do the job. The editor signed off with a personal pledge of a hundred dollars.

A weekly rehash of the article as well as a published list of contributors got the project off to a flying start. With the money, letters to the editor poured in, assenting to the high moral purpose of the paving job. Remembrance waxed ripe with the loosening of purse strings. Dr. and Mrs. So-and-so (her great, great grandfather fought with the Confederates) were happy to mail in their check for two hundred fifty dollars in honor of the brave men of *all* wars. Citizen X believed that warriors like Turner Ashby came from a mold now broken, but would be mended, he predicted, by future generations if they took a renewed interest in the furtherance of patriotism (he was good for fifty dollars). Local corporations were sure touches, especially ones with Jackson or Ashby in their names. Selflessly, schoolchildren parted with their allowances.

Whenever the mail-ins flagged, the stakes were raised. Contributors of more than one hundred dollars were told that their names would be listed at the site. Out-of-towners with the surname Ashby were invited to trace their genealogy to see if any hereditary lines dovetailed back to the general. A new and improved interpretive roadsign was promised, to replace the aging one that was growing indecipherable with peeling paint and dry rot. The banners were waved a little harder, the jingoism pitched a little further, and six months later the fund was over the top.

For all the good intentions that plagued the project from start to finish, I lament the final result. Here is not history preserved, but rather history layered over with yet another affront. The immediacy of a modern all-weather, machine-graded gravel lane is nothing on the order of a rutted wagon trail (or something similar, which approximated the original road to the monument), but it is better than a blank, crowned runway of asphalt. Pavement gets in the way of the senses. You travel too fast to see anything except that which is ahead of you. You travel too fast to smell, except the strong whiff of pollution that clouts you when the windows are rolled down. You perceive yourself bridging the valleys and cutting through the hills as you ride. A road so modified by levelness, by smoothness no longer imparts a feeling for topographic differentiation. On an interstate, this is probably a good thing; speed, after all, is the tamer of great distances. But on a road four-tenths of a mile long, leading to a supposed point of quiet contemplation, speed is unnecessary – not only unnecessary but also ridiculous.

In its essence, paving is killing. Killing acre after acre of ground with a heavy hydrocarbon night that smothers the toughest of weeds. Killing the soil's chance for absorption of rainfall. Killing the micro-ecology, killing the scenic potential, killing the remove from litter and fumes. I read somewhere that if all the pavement in the continental United States were joined together, it would cover an area as big as Georgia. That's a lot of ground to lay to waste – but of course it's not wasted. Imagine one unpaved iota of this, an expanse of red clay soaked by a rain or two, graded into a characteristically busy cloverleaf? It would look like a demolition derby. Muck and slipperiness are necessarily restricted to four-wheel-drive enthusiasts' pipedreams.

We have steel rails, we have corridors in the sky, but it is our road system that is king – and chief executioner. Or, to put it another way, paved thoroughfares are the trapfalls of our civilization. We endanger ourselves for the sake of connectedness. We pave, we rush, we cross the wasteland between points A and B with as close an approximation of instantaneousness as we can muster. We achieve fullness of being on our roads. It is difficult to imagine a time when roads were hoof- and wheel-paths shaped by the peculiarities of the countryside, indifferent to any concept of convenience and often impassable during bad weather. One of the more pervasive forms of road-love I notice as I drive along (see, I'm just *driving along* like everybody else) is the attention people pay to their driveways. The briefest traverse between roadway and garage (or carport, or parking apron) is given the full treatment; not only is it paved, its blackness is restored annually with a paint called "asphalt sealer," which comes in five-gallon buckets. Gents in jogging gear push long-handled brooms across their mini-interstates, brushing the pebbly canvases until they glow darkly. To conclude the ritual – and make the fruits of their labor perfectly clear to neighbors and passersby – these asphalt artists block the entrances to their driveways with the empty buckets. Keep off! Nobody (that includes you, Mom, with your trunkful of groceries) is permitted to sully the masterpiece as it dries.

Pavement is glorified in other ways. Painted arrows and elongated lettering shunt drivers to the left and right. No reason for road signs: let the pavement speak! Stripes, both yellow and white, are limned with dazzling effect, enhanced in places with raised reflectors. "Pay attention at night!" Speed bumps are installed in shopping centers. "Cool it, folks!" Then there are the pressure pads and assorted sensors to control traffic signals embedded within the road surface. Smart streets. The latest thing to do is to recycle worn pavement: strip off and pulverize the top inch or two, add fresh tar and nuggets of rubber from ground-up tires, and lay 'er down again. Full circle repavement, with the poetic justice of helping to reduce the mountains of discarded tires, a concurrent American dilemma.

The little lane to the monument didn't need to be a part of the big picture. As lightly traveled as it is, it could have remained gravel for another century or two. It could have stayed that way until the convention of rubber-tire-rolling-on-asphalt is long obsolete and the harnessing of anti-gravity is old hat. For, mark my words, the time will come when visitors to Civil War sites drop in from the sky. What will happen to the tens of thousands of square miles of pavement then? Will they be recycled vertically as skyscrapers for the indigent? Will they be dumped in the Marianas Trench?

In practical terms, paving the gravel road to the Ashby monument accomplished nothing. The historical site is no more (or less) accessible. Wayward minors still hang out there, playing music loudly, drinking beer, taking drugs. Serious students of the Civil War visit about as often as they did before. The radius of the newly paved turnaround between the trees is poorly engineered; car tires tend to veer off the asphalt platform as the turn is negotiated. The four-inch drop to earth gently jolts the senses. Having fallen to the safety net, the driver realizes that the spongy sensation of the leaf mold is a pleasant one, yet the brain has been programmed to respond negatively. Tires don't belong there. Dutifully, the driver torques the steering wheel and clambers back to the pavement.

The amenities that came with the paving job, as announced in the newspaper, include a single trash can (painted sky blue, which seems to be the preferred municipal trash can color these days), and the new sign relaying the "battle" particulars. The sign maker held nothing back, for beneath his nomenclature he took the trouble to render two Lilliputian armies about to attack each other across the whitewashed Masonite. The painted soldiers look rested and well fed. On the back of the sign, squarely facing the monument not fifty feet away, is a slurry of print listing the honored donors who gave more than anybody else did. This directory embodies a fastidiousness that contrasts with the coarse gray bark of the hardwoods. It overpowers the two dirty wreaths of plastic flowers somebody from the United Daughters of the Confederacy propped against the limestone cube. It adds to the crazy, mismatched at-

15

mosphere of the immediate viewshed – the transmission line pylons, the intruding noose of pavement, the blue barrel. Ashby couldn't have died here! Surely we are mistaken! Perhaps it happened over in the field next to the apartments, or farther up in the woods.

At any rate, the blight of the newspaper's crusade has settled over the spot – it has been truly brought up to date, and a lot of people feel good about what has transpired, having earmarked personal donations toward its end. From the start, I felt it to be an act of historical outrage, but I didn't breathe a word to anyone. I decided against posting my letter to the editor; I have submitted such letters before, only to be countered with printed hoots of derision. I waited in vain for someone else's letter to appear, a braver paragraph of dissent. Alas, the bandwagon was rolling jauntily; the coffers were filling as righteous pride swelled exponentially. My plan would have been to leave the gravel lane as it was, re-route the transmission line, erect a sign (somewhat smaller) that stuck to the facts of the skirmish. My plan would have focused on subtraction, rather than addition. My plan would have cost a repudiation or two, and a few ruffled feathers. But my plan didn't get off the drawing board because I didn't have the guts to present it. I didn't think anybody would be there to back me up in a public forum. I lacked the courage to be a voice crying in the wilderness.

I guess the fear of being branded a kook lies at the bottom of my usually brimming well of self-esteem. As an artist, I tend to be defensive when broadsided by critics. I know the let down of finding out that appreciation for one's work (or one's self) will never be forthcoming from certain individuals, no matter what. I also know the flash points in human discourse: when criticism turns into savaging, when dislike turns to distemper. I've met only one or two people in my entire life who think that gravel is superior to pavement. And so I backed off from causing an imbroglio, preferring to watch from the sidelines with a sad shaking of my head as the paving panoply unfolded.

Heraclitus, that Greek good ol' boy (born about 550 B.C.), taught his followers that *all is flux,* and proceeded to prove it by jumping in and out of a river, declaiming that he was both wet and dry at the same time. He preached that all things are really the same thing, the many are one, that differences are apparent only because of the constant flow from one state of being to another.

I apply this wisdom to the site of General Ashby's demise. With a trick of philosophical mirrors, it's still there, pristine as in 1862. An advance company of Union cavalry comes galloping over the hill. Ashby and his

16

fellow cavalrymen guarding the rear of Jackson's columns of infantry are caught in momentary repose, but they mount quickly and form a countercharge. The skirmish materializes, intensifies. Seeing that his steed is wounded, Ashby swings down from the saddle, takes a few steps, and is dispatched to oblivion. Pry up the pavement, his blood may still be wet.

THREE

The best way to preserve a battleground that was farmed in the 1860s is to keep farming it. Stewardship of land is at its most conscientious if the profit motive isn't far beneath the surface of the steward's good intentions. Coming to our forty acres of rolling hayfields and realizing that I would be the one responsible for their care, I decided to develop the necessary farming skills: to make the hay myself and sell it by the bale from the barn to local customers—small-time farmers and animal fanciers who raised a few horses or cows. I set about the gradual acquisition of haymaking equipment, scouring the countryside for used implements that could be pulled by my Kubota tractor, an orange work-pony that had been in my possession for more than a decade. The sickle mower, windrowing rake, baler, and haywagon that I collected were basic necessities, a sort of starter set in the business of hay farming.

And then I went to work. But, despite my preference for low-budget, low-impact agricultural methods, it was clear after one season that the potential for greater profit warranted some streamlining of the operation. Like any businessperson, I harbored dreams of expansion—dreams that were grounded in the balance sheet at the end of the year and the tax deductions. To preserve my penchant for making hay—that is, for taking the trouble to mow it, rake it, bale it, and transport it to the barn—I needed to be more efficient with my time. Farming singlehandedly, and generating a modest profit of several thousand dollars a year for my effort, I could scarcely afford the total and tedious immersion my starter set required of me.

The first thing I needed was a second tractor. Not a towering beast of burden, as my neighbors had in their farm fleets, but a general purpose, or utility tractor with about twice the drawbar strength of the twenty-one-horsepower Kubota. To Becky, I was uttering heresy, as I had given her my solemn assurance that the Kubota would suit my needs now and forever. After the first full haymaking season, however, I had to renege on my pledge. Circumstances had changed. Making three thousand bales of hay took mechanical muscle, more than could be coaxed from the little Japanese diesel, which had never burned a drop of oil for years, but now, revving to the red line, consumed a quart of oil a day. It seemed unwise to overwork the tractor, just as it seemed inexpedient to subject myself to a cross-my-fingers, yes-I-can ordeal each time I drove out to the field. Besides, the tractor's lack of a *live* power take-off, or PTO, that turned independently of the drivetrain, restricted its adaptability to haymaking equipment.

My quest for a second tractor led me through Virginia, West Virginia, Maryland, and Pennsylvania—wherever promising advertisements originated. Like used cars, used farming machines are frequently traded out of state. Looking for the right piece of equipment can consume fruitless months and miles, but there is an education to be gained in the looking. By inspecting all kinds of farm tractors that came up short of my requirements for one reason or another, I was able to visualize the ideal tractor. And as luck would have it, I discovered that tractor right in downtown Harrisonburg at the White (formerly Oliver) dealership. My belated find was a 1967 Oliver 550 with a forty-two-horsepower gas engine, live PTO, and 2400 hours on its tachourmeter. Having been sold new and serviced in the interim by the same dealer, its dependability was unimpeachable. It was a creampuff of a tractor. Since the end of the 1960s, through the 1970s, and into the 1980s, it had been run—on an average—less than a hundred hours a year.

In general appearance (code words for desirability), the tractor looked its age. Its green paint was faded, its tires were nearly treadless. Oil that seeped at the gaskets and engine seals had long been transmuted into grime. Grease nipples were stalactites of crud. Yet there were subtle hints of care, of preservation, about the old tractor which set it apart from the other candidates I had recently looked over. There was no play in its steering wheel. The plastic insignia (a black and orange shield) on the steering hub was intact, and all dashboard gauges were in working order, their glass unbroken. Even the cigarette lighter worked.

My fondness for older tractors is based on a practical as well as an aesthetic judgment. Yesteryear's tractors cost less, look better, run better, and last longer. Their sturdiness, their no-frills stereotype contrasts starkly with the contemporary equivalent. To me, the older machines represent a vanished agrarian ethos, reflecting a time when grilles and fenders conveyed an amour propre which seemed to say, "I toil, but I am something to look at, too." Farm machinery connoisseurs still regard the Oliver 550 as an outstanding utility tractor. Compact yet powerful, it was the culmination of a model line that underwent numerous improvements over twenty years, only to be terminated in the early 1970s when Oliver was phased out of existence by its new owner, White Motor Corporation.

Locally, there are many 550s still in use, as well as their predecessors, the Super 55s. From the 1930s through the 1960s, Oliver had been the fourth largest manufacturer of agricultural equipment in the world (after John Deere, Ford, and International Harvester). With headquarters in Chicago and plants throughout the midwest, Oliver's roots went back to the earliest days of progressive farming. Its farm tractor division in Charles City, Iowa, was a direct descendant of the Oliver Chilled Plow Company, which sold the first mass-produced, horse- or mule-drawn iron-bladed plows that turned under the virgin prairie during the mid-nineteenth-century westward expansion. In 1929, Oliver merged with the Hart-Parr Company, the originator of internal combustion farm tractors, also in Charles City. (One of the earliest Hart-Parr machines, old No. 3, currently resides in the Smithsonian's Museum of American Technology.) In 1906, the word "tractor" was added to the English language by W. H. Williams, sales manager for Hart-Parr, who decided that the words "gasoline traction engine" were too cumbersome for advertising copy. When Hart-Parr joined Oliver Plow, two manufacturers of threshing and seeding equipment were included in the deal. The conglomerate called itself the Oliver Corporation.

The Crash of 1929 threatened the merger, but sales of the product line remained stable throughout the years of the Great Depression. Ironically, the corporation's Achilles heel was its advertising. In print, the pitch wasn't strident enough. Neon signs over the dealerships weren't as compelling as they could have been. Sales strategy was based upon reputation and word of mouth: Oliver sold and serviced "The Finest In Farm Machinery." Indeed, the Oliver Corporation had been responsible for a number of important innovations. It was the first to put pneumatic tires on farm tractors. It pioneered (with the Cleveland Tractor Company, a subsidiary) the production of lightweight crawlers for farm and orchard use. It initiated the "new look," i.e., deco streamlining (for example, the fully enclosed engine shroud), which lead to an industry-wide re-tooling for sheet metal. The problem was that quantitative jumps in unit sales were never forthcoming. By the late 1940s, Oliver was clearly lagging in the postwar hustle to mechanize agriculture. Two decades later, after White Motor Corporation had leveraged its way into ownership, Semon "Bunkie" Knudsen, then president of White, sounded the death knell for what he perceived to be an unprofitable manufacturing arm.

When Oliver closed its plants in the early 1970s, one of the most trusted names in agriculture passed into history. The simultaneous failures of other long-established farm equipment manufacturers created a vacuum that was soon filled by products from Asia and Europe. By the mid-1980s, in the face of increasingly stiff foreign competition, only four North American companies still produced farm tractors—White, Case-International, Ford, and John Deere ("the *other* green tractor," as Oliver aficionados say). Each of these companies sells Asian- or European-assembled "low end" tractors (sixty horsepower or less) and replacement parts. White has since gone kaput, and in the near future only tractors of a hundred horsepower and above will display the "Made in U.S.A" sticker.

The Oliver 550 harks back to an era when the export of American agricultural technology was the norm, a technology that spared no details and cut no corners. But it was also an era when American manufacturers were plagued by recessions, layoffs, and aging plants that ultimately forced them to concede rich market opportunities. Foreign manufacturing giants like Kubota were able to fill orders faster and cheaper. While American companies wallowed in tried-and-true design and production methods, their competitors across the ocean implemented innovative technologies that stretched materials pound for pound and revolutionized assembly lines. An American tractor was built to last fifty years; until the sting of competition was felt, it hardly mattered that the steel in one tractor could go for two, or even three, or that the assembly line on which the tractors were built was bloated with the over-regimentation of union labor.

In most ways, the 550 is a paragon of stolidity. It looks like a bulldog and drives like a Mack truck. Its engine sits within a wraparound cast-iron cradle frame beneath a hood that curves at the sides like a mansard roof. Its steering wheel is an oversized, prominently knuckled circle of bakelite that empowers the operator with a sense of purpose. Out in front, above the sturdy swivel-axle, the tractor's fiberglass grille delineates a dozen hollow rectangles, the leading edge upright as if boldly to proclaim, "Air intake!" But the grille is a telling example of what went wrong as American agricultural manufacturing began its competitive decline. The grille *looks* good, but it wasn't designed to withstand the rigors of farming. A token space-age material, fiberglass was an up-to-date substitute for stamped metal, but its application here turns out to be uncharacteristically frail.

The tractor's rudimentary rear fenders, upon which teardrop-shaped headlights are perched (as well as a single work light to the rear), are pie-shaped wedges balanced on the rear axle. A comparison to the Kubota's fender-tire ratio is worth noting; in the same time frame, the Japanese were designing fenders like big ears, imparting a *trompe l'oeil* massiveness to their machines. However, the Oliver's transmission/differential case is generously proportioned, and flanged and bolted as prolifically as a diving bell. One wonders what enormous stresses the engineers had in mind when they drew up the plans. The drivetrains of two Japanese tractors could be stuffed into such a repository; it takes five gallons of gear oil to fill.

But the 550's *pièce de résistance* is surely its seat. This is a sculpted steel pan cantilevered forward by a linkage of jointed arms and flexing rubber, wide and deep enough to cradle the broadest backside. Without padding, it makes a regal perch. I have made a study of tractor seats and their comparative comfort, and while I have found one or two equals to the Oliver throne (with simpler suspensions, such as a single automotive-type shock absorber and a coil spring), I haven't found anything that exceeds its cushioning effect. The Oliver Corporation must have patented the system. When I climb onto the tractor and position myself squarely in the seat—thus depressing it about halfway—my posterior floats as if on a cloud. Comfort in the field far exceeds what I experience on the Kubota, which has an unsprung, ungenerous seat-pan fastened to the drivetrain housing with two rubber grommets, both long since compressed. I am thankful for the ergometric savvy of the bygone engineering staff in Iowa. They took into account a farmer's most tender anatomical feature.

I purchase the 550 in the fall, too late to put it to use with haymaking. Instead, I tackle a project I've been putting off for several years—cleaning up derelict fencelines. Long ago, the forty acres were divided into small pasturages, the borders of which are now demarcated by linear humps along the ground, raised and roughened areas booby-trapped with cedar stumps and rogue strands of barbed wire. Farmers accreted them with their plowshares, over and over, and then, between growing seasons, the hooves of perambulating cattle pounded them firm. The process went on right until Becky and I bought the place, at which time the cattle were removed.

By leveling the humps, I can make four large hayfields from eight smaller ones. This is a worthy goal because it will save me time and labor during haymaking, as well as reduce wear and tear on my machinery. Oblique turning at field corners takes its toll on universal joints, ball joints, skid plates, tires. The fewer turns I make, the faster I can work. It makes sense to steer a straight course for as long as possible instead of hauling on the steering wheel every couple hundred feet—and slipping the clutch and disengaging the PTO and manipulating the hydraulic lever.

Earl, my friend who operates heavy equipment, is ready to contribute the brawn of his front-end loader that will be necessary for the heavy digging and rough grading, and yet I hesitate. The preservationist within me recoils from altering the battlefield terrain. I don't want to destroy any border configuration that might have existed in 1862, even though I have no way of ascertaining how the pastures were arranged back then. No posts or boards remain; they were ripped out fifteen years earlier, when the farmer who sold us the land switched from tillage to cattle grazing. He has no idea of the age of the field divisions either, although he reminisces about how his cows used to ensnare themselves in the barbed wire. What remnants of wire I come across are decidedly modern, rusting evidence of late fixes.

My best clue to the divisions' antiquity is a locust post and barbed wire cross-fence that jogs through the center of our property. This fence line was in disrepair until Van and I patched it one spring in preparation for a horse that Hope was temporarily boarding. I am reasonably certain that it dates from the present century; it is old, but not old enough to be of Civil War vintage. If it were that old, the chances are it would be a rail fence—also called a worm, or snake fence—but in these environs, a fence of such antiquity would probably have been destroyed during the war itself, when collecting firewood was a prime objective at the conclusion of a day's march. Fence rails made ready fuel for soldiers craving the semblance of a hot meal, or at least a cup of tea. At the start of his Shenandoah Valley campaign, Stonewall Jackson had adamantly opposed rail burning; he deemed it a punishable offense in all but the most desperate of circumstances, when he reluctantly permitted the plunder. Later on, when times got harder, Confederate soldiers, like their Union counterparts, burned fence rails with impunity.

So the more I think about it, I'm convinced that my quibbles are overblown. There is no documentable imperative to preserve the bothersome humps. Still, when I give Earl the go ahead, I consider borrowing a metal detector just in case . . . but no, my conscience overrules. I remind myself that I am philosophically opposed to rooting out battle artifacts (I won't allow anyone else to root them out either). If the loader turns up something, I will rebury it with dignity. Nevertheless, I keep a sharp lookout while the loader bucket bites into the earth. At one place, not far from the barn, a nest of copperheads is exposed—the first snakes I've seen on the property. While I shovel-whack the wriggling mass, my attention is momentarily diverted, but I stick to my archeological mandate. The former fence lines yield no treasure.

When Earl is done, I finish the grading with the 550 and a rear-mounted scraper blade. The Oliver's left-handed shift feels unfamiliar; my right hand keeps seeking out a shift knob that isn't there. The tractor's weight and horsepower are several orders of magnitude beyond that to which I am accustomed; I can actually rip up a bladeful of dirt without spinning the tires. By the time the ground is worked flat, snow flurries are blowing in from the west. I climb down and tramp over the bare dirt with a hand-cranked seed broadcaster hugged to my chest. Snow and seed mingle on the wind. The rusted gears of the seeder make a lonesome squeal beneath the gray, socked-in sky. I exhale visible clouds. The former fence lines are truly disappearing, faster than I can imagine. The battlefield lies smooth and uninterrupted beneath a spectral dusting of white.

FOUR

Sitting on a slowly rolling tractor, directing an obstreperous farm implement along an interminable row, I allow my mind to range across vignettes from my past. I have come to this magisterial perch by a strangely circuitous route; it could not be said that I was born to farm. In truth, nothing in my upbringing or education (aside from the fact that I played with farm toys) pointed to a predilection for agrarian self-employment.

I joined this world from a brick-bungalowed suburb of Washington, D.C., as World War II was peaking. Franklin D. Roosevelt was in the White House, the war effort mobilized the resources of the nation, and refugee physicists were unfurling a top secret, billion-dollar blueprint called the Manhattan Project. My mother and father, an unlikely pair of former graduate students (Columbia University '39) who had courted beneath the Trilon and Perisphere in Flushing Meadows, were four years into a marriage that had already produced one daughter and would produce—soon after I came along—a second son.

Both my mother and father had tremendous personal ambition that got sidetracked by the exigencies of the Depression years. My mother was the only child of second-generation New Yorkers who aspired to culture and gentility but lost everything in increments—money, marriage, and good health. My father, the son of a plumber in Newark, New Jersey, was a gifted schoolboy who rebelled against his working class roots almost as soon as he learned to read. Both my parents had troubled adolescences, largely inflicted by family jealousies. Both began college—he to study architecture, she to flounder in pre-med before switching to a major in English—as a means of escaping their unhappy home situations. Then both dropped out because neither could afford the tuition while their families were counting on them for support. Despite the interruptions, both managed to earn undergraduate degrees. By the time they met in graduate school (a furthering of education that I have always interpreted as an extension of their flight from home), both had embraced a new field of study: sociology. When I ponder their mutual choice, the theoretical examination of social systems, I see not only a reflection of the times—the calling-forth of a soon-to-be-shattered brave new world, as glimpsed in the fantasies of the 1939 World's Fair—but also the determination to climb out of the confusing cauldron of their respective upbringings. They were amassing the knowledge to do better when it came to raising their own children.

In wartime Washington, my father worked as a lower-level bureaucrat in the Department of Labor—this, because he had been granted a deferment as a married man with dependents. My mother was a housewife. Sociology seems to have fallen by the wayside. My parents became typical white, middle-class exponents of the American success story. My father planted a victory garden. My mother strolled the latest infant in a lacquered, navy-blue buggy. My father bought a second-hand baby grand piano and relaxed at the end of the day with self-taught tinkling. My mother took innumerable black and white snapshots with the family Kodak. In the driveway sat their beetle-backed Ford sedan, unused for weeks because of gas rationing.

My earliest memory of Takoma Park, Maryland, is of falling off a wall in the backyard. It was a low brick retaining wall, no big deal, but my few fledgling steps along it had ended in disaster. Another early memory is of a sky filled with airplanes, droning military transports and bombers, which my mother told me much later was a show of strength and sorrow above the nation's capital the day Roosevelt died.

At the conclusion of the war, my father opted to leave government service because he felt stifled by (and was passed up for promotion because of) bureaucratic in-fighting—a situation that would plague him during his subsequent career as a college professor of management and economics. My father was an indefatigable team player and later an excellent teacher, but he compartmentalized his personality. At heart, he had an artistic streak (he painted, composed music, made ceramics, wrote poetry, and so forth) that found expression at the borders of his professional life, but try as he might, he was unable to integrate these remarkable outpourings with the more mundane skills of a career achiever. Artistically, he never allowed himself to blossom; his creative bent, by far the deepest, most soulful manifestation of his personality, remained second fiddle to his public persona. Muzzled for long periods, the volcano within vented itself, sometimes explosively.

28

My mother embodied frustration of a different kind. She wanted to work in public — her advanced degree made her eminently qualified — but she denied herself the opportunity. Her first duty was to her family, she believed, and so she went about her housekeeping in an aggrieved way: banging the vacuum cleaner on the legs of furniture, overcooking vegetables in the pressure cooker, browbeating my sister, my brother, and me to better ourselves, take our baths, turn out our lights. She was a victim of propriety. Married women of her generation didn't escape their households unless an act of God intervened. In the quiet corner of an upstairs room, she retreated to her desk and committed the hours between duties and meals to *belles lettres*. She wrote short fiction, novels, travelogues, poetry. (Interestingly, for a time during their courtship my mother and father communicated by sonnet — *godawful* stuff that embarrassed the hell out of me in later years when I was made privy to the ribbon-tied packets.) Aside from the stray poem that found its way into print in her college alumni magazine or at the bottom of an editorial page of a newspaper (*The New York Times,* as I recall, accepted a couple) her work went unpublished. She never pressed hard enough, never pushed her talent to its logical extreme. It was not considered ladylike. Her fictional characters were cloche-headed, somewhat demure college girls who fell in love (on a steamship, on a train) with older men in tweeds. My mother, too, subsumed the creative person at the core of her being for someone who effused responsibility and decorum.

And so I was the middle child of a failed artist and a failed writer, although on the surface, my parents were successful, engaging people. What was hidden from relatives, neighbors, and acquaintances was not hidden from me. I witnessed the secret plodding toward success — my mother pecking at her Hermes portable typewriter in deepest concentration, and my father's infrequent sessions at the easel, during which he became an altogether different person, a fanatic of paint tubes and turpentine.

After my father quit his job in Washington, he worked briefly at the office of the War Assets Administration in Cleveland, Ohio. Our family moved into a two-story walkup beside the freight yards of the Nickel Plate. It was there I was given my first toy train — a windup engine, boxcar, flatcar, and caboose that ran on a circular track. Reality and its simulacrum chugged vociferously all day long. My father's duties at the WAA were by their very nature self-destructing; nine months later he was out of a job. Our family was financially forced to make a temporary retreat to Lake Lackawanna, New Jersey, where my paternal grandparents owned a cottage. During a mostly snowbound winter there, my father sat at his drafting board and produced wallpaper patterns he hoped to market to an industrial design firm in New York City. His work was turned down. Halfheartedly, he switched to painting a winterscape or two—paintings I remember because of their wanly lit depictions of snowdrifts, blanketed eaves, and smoke-curling chimneys. I came down with a bad case of tonsillitis and had a tonsillectomy at the Parsippany Hospital. I was three at the time, the youngest patient in a ward full of war veterans who indefatigably plied me with chocolate bars. In the meantime one of my father's employment feelers was panning out; his former boss in Cleveland had joined the administrative faculty of the University of Rhode Island and was offering him an instructorship in business management there. It was the lowest-paid faculty position, but a position nonetheless. He accepted immediately.

We moved east to Rhode Island, relocating to one end of a provisional barracks at Fort Kearney, a recently abandoned military installation on Narragansett Bay. Due to the postwar housing shortage and the GI multitudes enrolled at the state university, it was the only available place to live. Although I was barely four years old, I remember Fort Kearney in detail: its sea mists, its concrete seawalls, its knoll-like ammunition bunkers, its rusting artillery emplacements and embankments (the guns had been removed, but it didn't take much imagination to put them back). Broken life rafts and other naval detritus regularly washed ashore. It was an amazing place, the spiritual antithesis of a freight yard. Its plain, asbestos-sided buildings with peaked green roofs all related to each other in function and design. One row of barracks was said to have housed German prisoners of war. There was enough *fort-ness* left to feel the residue of the military presence, even though a civilian lassitude was setting in. The place could be positively spooky under certain atmospheric conditions—a ghost fort. Just enough time had elapsed so that the dark green paint of the barracks' trim was peeling and the storm-worn roof shingles, sloughing their emerald grit, were beginning to curl. Weeds populated the cracks in the pavement, and beach grasses waved thickly around the fortifications.

My appreciation for the beauty of nature must have begun at Fort Kearney. I loved everything about the place. The moods of the bay—its gray, gloomy chop, its shimmering sun reflection—encouraged my most abstruse thoughts. The surf that pounded the rocks and washed over the tidal pools tugged at the very essence of my being. The smell of the sea breeze exhilarated me. I could have grown up there forever.

30

As it turned out, we lived at Fort Kearney for less than a year. My parents hated it there. Our family of five was crowded into three beaverboard-walled rooms (randomly broached with nail holes) that were heated with a single kerosene stove. Sanitary conditions were questionable. The fort was home to married students as well as recently arrived college faculty, so babies and dogs, not to mention raucous parties on weekends, marred the quietude of sea contemplation. For two weeks in the winter my father was desperately ill with measles; and then my mother caught it, which brought family life to a standstill. When a farmhouse between Narragansett and Wakefield came vacant in late spring, my parents moved us out on short notice and never looked back.

The Old Whaley House, as it was called, was a spacious and underfurnished saltbox that stood on a plain behind a salt marsh, still close enough to the sea to smell it. The rent was too high for it to serve as other than a transient residence. I remember its backyard as being an expanse of goldenrod and rabbit's foot clover. My most prominent memory, however, is of a large, completely white spider walking across my bedroom floor. Whether the arachnid had recently crawled out of a flour bin or a paint can, I will never know. (I have been told, on good authority, that albino spiders dwell almost exclusively in caves.)

Not many months later, my parents bought the first of two houses in Kingston and West Kingston, locales we were to dwell in for the better part of a decade. The initial purchase was a bathroomless tenant shack down the road from the university dairy, near the turf plots of the agricultural station. Its charm (and price) as a fixer-upper strongly appealed to my father, who in later years always spoke fondly of "The House on the Plains" as though it were his Shangri-la. It stood in the middle of a superannuated two-acre apple orchard, behind which was a potato field. Its appurtenances included an outhouse, a chicken coop, and a tool shed. As money came available, a bathroom and a furnace were installed, insulation was stuffed in the walls, storm windows were added, and some interior partitioning was done.

During the few years we lived in this first house of our own it was transformed into something quite comfortable, even cozy. Its location was conducive to childhood wanderlust. My sister, my brother, and I claimed fiefdoms in the apple trees and outbuildings. We scavenged for potatoes in the fall after the mechanical harvester had dug up the ground. In summer we swam in Thirty Acre Pond, the pumping source for the agricultural station, and in winter we sledded in the hollow of a field across the road, where a mysterious, locked root cellar lay half buried.

We watched the cows as they were being milked at the dairy, and I fell in love with Louise, the dairyman's daughter. (Her face and hands always seemed a little dirty, appealingly so; she spent a good deal of time helping her dad with chores.) On Sundays we'd sneak over to cavort on the turf plots—verdant carpets with lushly living pile. I learned to ride my sister's bicycle—a sky blue, fat-wheeled Montgomery-Ward catalog offering that my father assembled with much cursing the night before her seventh or eighth birthday. One day as I was pedaling into the wind along the road toward campus (past the dairy) I was actually blown to a stop. I didn't weigh enough to keep myself in motion.

I went to nursery school at the University of Rhode Island in the Watson House, an ancient farmhouse still preserved between sidewalks and ivy-covered classroom buildings. It was there I became a builder. The school was run by student teachers supervised by a family friend, a polio victim who played the zither. In the mornings, I'd use oversized wooden play blocks to build towers that my teachers left standing until my parents could inspect them at the end of the day. Block by block I'd construct my ceiling-scrapers, but I have no recollection of ever tearing them down; dismantling always occurred after I had gone home. The next morning, finding the blocks neatly stowed in boxes, I'd resign myself to building anew.

If my teachers were worried about my exclusionary play, they never said a word to me. Erecting the tall, precipitously balanced structures became a kind of duty. It was expected that I impress peers and adults alike on a daily basis, although there were other, more communal facets of nursery school that I enjoyed just as much. I loved games of tag and hide-and-seek. I loved milk-and-cookie breaks (milk came from the dairy in half-pint bottles stamped in blue with the University Seal). I loved communal naps.

But the thing I loved most of all was participating in the rhythm band. At least once a day we were all gathered in a circle, teachers included, and given something to shake or rattle or bang. To the accompaniment of the zither, one of the teachers would sing, or we'd all sing, but it was the making of the rhythm that captivated me. Slapping a tambourine, clanging a pot with a spoon, striking one stick against another—adding to the primitive, unison beat with syncopation either artful or inept was a pleasure beyond compare. To any listener it must have seemed we made an insane racket, but to me, it was building of another kind, a phrasing and punctuation that made a space for everyone, an introductory lesson in the universal kinship of music.

In kindergarten, at Kingston grammar school, I threw beanbags at the ceiling, leaving marks on the acoustic tile, for which I was repeatedly reprimanded. Solitary block building was no longer encouraged. In its stead, I fixed my concentration on the wooden cars and trucks and airplanes that jumbled the toy box—tough, polychromed rolling stock that could be sat on and kicked around. But the sharing of toys was mandatory now, and it was not beyond me to throw possessive tantrums. The only activity I thoroughly enjoyed was fingerpainting. In this I excelled, but the sessions were brief. The best activities always came with the strictest time constraints. I did not withhold my disapproval. I probably whined. All in all the kindergarten teacher, Mrs. Streeter, found my behavior problematic; she complained to my parents, who in turn put pressure on me to loosen my grip on my fantasies. I was exhorted time and again to get along with everybody else, to initiate that dichotomy between the private and public side of my personality. The halter of approval was slipped over my head, the bit of conformity shoved succinctly into my mouth. I was urged to become captive of the good opinion of others.

When I moved up the half-flight of stairs to the first-grade room of the Kingston schoolhouse, I was highly motivated to get some learning done. This was a real classroom with desks, inkwells, and blackboards. As old-fashioned as I picture the room today—with its oiled floor, its varnished wainscoting and woodwork, its flag in the corner, its portraits of George and Martha like overseers above the blackboard, its chain-suspended yellow-globed lights (tombs for dead flies), its mullioned windows with pairs of roller shades installed at the sash junction so that the topmost shade pulled upward on a squealing arrangement of pulleys—it brings back quintessential feelings of pride. I remember how mature it made me feel. I had left the romper room for good.

My teacher, Mrs. Fitzgerald, a heavyset stereotype with a frayed bun of gray hair, was a businesslike disciplinarian not without a sympathetic heart. She didn't countenance shenanigans of any kind. Her job was to teach, not babysit. She shouldered a moral imperative. In my eighteen-plus years of schooling, I have studied under more elegant teachers, more inspiring teachers, and certainly more ingratiating teachers, but I never had a better *teacher*. She was the standard; she imparted the three R's as steadily and systematically as the ticking of the Roman-numeraled clock to the right of Martha and George. Mrs. Fitzgerald was responsible for the foundation on which the airy castle of higher education would sit, and she intended it to be built of solid stone. *She didn't put up with any tomfoolery.* If a youngster fell behind in his or her understanding of the simplest undertaking—how to spell "cat," how to add two plus two—she took it upon herself to correct the problem. She had uncanny powers of focus. When she looked at me, she looked directly inside my brain. She knew the importance of rote. She made us memorize everything we learned. Nobody, not even the so-called dummies, could escape her ladle of knowledge. The class moved ahead as one.

She was the perfect antidote to kindergarten. She was benevolent in a way you couldn't take advantage of. I don't remember why, but at the time I had a great need to carry around a little green tractor—a ten-cent plastic toy that fit in my pocket. Naturally, such playthings weren't allowed at school (this was before the days of show-and-tell), but Mrs. Fitzgerald sensed my mental and/or emotional predicament, and since I was one of her better students (at least I had no learning problem) she let me bring it, *provided that it stayed in my pocket.* The only time I dared to disobey her was when I was in the boys' room. In the beaded-board stall with the door shut, I sat on the oak horseshoe beneath the copper-lined oak tank that was fastened to the wall six feet above my head and rolled that tractor to my heart's delight around every surface within reach. Periodically, I pulled the chain that released a slurping cascade down the pipe and into the porcelain bowl. I tried to keep my visits short but frequent, timing them to realistic intervals so as not to arouse suspicion. On one occasion, though, I stayed too long. Mrs. Fitzgerald came marching in, yanking open the door with glowering disapproval.

"Young man," she bellowed, "I *knew* what you were up to!" Meekly, I buttoned up and stowed the tractor back in my pocket. She never took the toy away from me, nor did she make a public spectacle of me for the class's edification. I, in turn, learned to confine my hands-on agrarian daydreams to after school and weekends. Not many weeks later, I stopped bringing my little tractor to school altogether. Mrs. Fitzgerald had the power to cure a stubborn neurosis.

Looking back on those first six years, I recognize a need to sift through the mass of my experiences, to cull a few important ones so that I can savor the best, the most worthy of preservation. My aim is most definitely not to wallow in nostalgia. As an adult homing in on the half-century mark, I find that certain experiences from my distant past leap off the pages, while others (many others) are like skipped pages, and still others are but blank spaces in the text of time. My childhood is a multi-volumed book that sits on the shelf, dusty and unread. If I were house-cleaning or moving to smaller accommodations, which volumes would I discard and which would I keep? What would I preserve of early childhood memories and influences? To what might I refer in the future, now that I've been expanding the reference library for so long?

I won't preserve the spankings and slappings—not to be confused with that contemporary catch-all called child abuse—simply because they weren't particularly effective. (Mrs. Fitzgerald's approach of reprimand and drill, combined with Herculean patience, got better results—shame being nobody's teacher.) I won't preserve the fun-and-games mentality of kindergarten, which, as an introduction to group dynamics, sought to flatten out individual differences and individuality itself. I'll also throw out those adult efforts of coercion that tried to make me a clone of an ideal youngster—the Procrustean theory of child rearing. And I won't keep the painful and humiliating accidents that couldn't be avoided—learning to wait for the bathroom, learning to not wet the bed.

I'll preserve the sense of self-worth that allows a child to say *I can* and *I am not afraid*. I'll preserve my innocent love for Louise Knight, whose thick black pigtails bobbed like musical notation against the tile walls of the milking parlor. I'll keep the uncontrollable smile that spread across my face as I pounded away in the rhythm band, and I'll keep the initial thrill of authority in my role as engineer of that windup train. Above all, I'll keep my uninhibited wonder at things as they appeal to my separate senses. It may sound like the affirmation of a fool, but I'll continue to do my best to stay child-like.

FIVE

I HAVE GIVEN MYSELF the title President of the Pond. Frivolous as it sounds, I am perfectly serious about the self-appointment. I may be the most hands-off, laissez-faire chief executive imaginable, with a short attention span and a predilection for losing my thread of thought, but I make a determined effort to discharge my duties. I have no cabinet of trusted advisors, no agenda, no regular schedule that relates to farm pond business. Weeks go by when I don't even visit the pond, although I do keep tabs on it from a distance. Depending on the rainfall and the rate of evaporation, the water level fluctuates regardless of my ministrations. The fish, the frogs, the muskrats, the water fowl all go about their routines with minimum intervention on my part.

The President of the Pond's seat of office is a chair on the edge of the earthen dam. In the heat of summer I go there, but I am loath to sit for long. Instead, I strip off my clothes and jump off the end of the dock. In the dead of winter I exchange my work boots for a pair of figure skates, baggage from my college days in New England, and draw with my whole being upon the ice. Swimming or skating, I use the pond to preserve my passion for sport, which began as satisfaction in my own strength and speed but is now a distant ripple from the stone's throw of youth—a tithe to the church of cardiovascular fitness.

The President's job requires plenty of attentive work, too. All year long, I remove floating debris from the trash rack that covers the standpipe. From early spring through late fall, I mow the grass on the dam and its adjacent spillway. I sickle the weeds that crowd around the dock where it joins the dam slope, and I clip blackberry bushes and sumac that threaten to overrun everywhere else. I also pick up dead limbs that have fallen in the water or on the ground. Eight years ago, during the pond's construction, five or six large trees, mostly hardwood, were fatally traumatized. The trees gradually dismember as each windy day or thunderstorm brings a few more limbs down, some of which require tractor and chain to haul away.

As President of the Pond, I am a fixer of things as they need fixing. If a board comes loose on the dock planking, I will see that it is renailed. If a sweet gum or wild cherry sapling gains a toehold at the water's edge—its roots a potential threat to the dam's integrity—I will see that it is yanked out. In the past year, the explosion of the muskrat population precipitated a crisis that called for presidential intervention. A portion of the dam just below water level was riddled with burrows and entrances, and in one place the excavations went right through to the other side. As the subterranean caverns collapsed one by one, the height of the dam dropped. Flood waters could have broached then, and that would have spelled disaster: the whole thing could have washed downstream.

As usual, Earl was called in for remedial earth moving. Meanwhile, Van and I set in place almost sixty feet of side armor, steel "diamond" mesh that extended both above and below the waterline. In addition, we trapped and shot as many of the water rodents as we could. (When a president goes to war, the righteous crusade is best carried through to the bitter end, including the mopping up.) The muskrats were thwarted, and to this day they are somewhat decreased in number.

But peace is my abiding preoccupation as I sit in my pond-side chair. I preside over the half-acre body of water as magnanimously as I possibly can. The pond and its ravine give privacy and shade to a quarter-mile leg of the rhomboid that comprises our forty acres. It takes a couple of minutes to walk there from our house, straight across a hayfield and down a bank at once tangled and bejeweled with wild blooms. With Earl's help, I built the pond shortly after we bought the land, even before I built the house. I waited in suspense as the pond slowly filled, and later I watched with disgust as algae, then duckweed encroached upon the water's surface. Overly rich nutrient runoff is the culprit—a problem that plagues most ponds in the Shenandoah Valley. The vegetative invasion waxes and wanes seasonally as farmers fertilize their fields and dispose of animal wastes. There is nothing the President can do about it. At its worst, in the height of summer, the algae resembles bank-to-bank Astroturf, although there are days when it partially or even totally disappears. Wind often blows the algal mass into a corrugated concentration at one end of the pond; at other times the green cover seems to vanish of its own accord, as if some epic of nature suddenly removes it from sight.

Of scientific reasons and rhythms I am mostly ignorant. The transfigurations of algae must be well known to an agronomist or botanist, and I'm sure, too, that somewhere in the scientific community there are people enumerating the practical uses of algae, just as Booker T. Washington enumerated the practical uses of peanuts. My role as chief executive restricts my interest in research. I can't delve too far into the reason for something when the mystery of the thing itself is what really captivates me. When I'm observing the pond I am a prisoner of my senses, and I like it that way. I try to limit my inquiries to empirical appreciation, like the great blue heron that perches on an outermost dock post and limes a jagged sunburst on the planking below.

I walk to the pond in a variety of moods. At my contemplative best, I am an eager absorber of the precise moment of the day, whether it be sunrise or sunset, high noon or full moon. I convey myself to the plastic chair—a household outcast now too mildewed, too ablated by the elements to be brought indoors—and simply look around. To all appearances, I am like a park-bench sitter, a sojourner in solitude. In actuality, of course, I am an inordinate busybody, entranced by everything that's going on, a scintillating screenful of pixels. Vicariously, I join in the fun. I add my lusty call to the chorus of frogs, I dart with the bass and bluegill, I park myself in a stationary swarm of gnats. I spin webs with the spiders. Sitting there and immersing myself in every activity that touches my clothed and bespectacled element, I think my humanity must be writ as large as a billboard. My guess is that the creatures in my presence think of me as a hot-breathed, strongly scented behemoth whose gawky limbs create disturbances in the air. To the freshwater denizens, I am a warm-blooded interloper momentarily at rest. There is nothing presidential about me. Conversely, from the human perspective, you could say that I am one with nature.

But sometimes I go down to the pond in other moods. Once in a while, I'm angrier than hell. I'm smarting from some stupid quarrel with Becky, or a painting gone bad, or an imagined personal slight, or any number of other monkey wrenches flung from time to time into the cogs of a serene disposition. The path through the hayfields is my escape route. I fling myself into the chair and feel as if the world has done me irreparable wrong. I hang my head like a figure from Picasso's blue period. The upsetting of my even keel leaves me vulnerable to the blackest of moods. Because of the circumstances, my presidential duties are temporarily suspended, yet like a buoyant tide, the quietude of the pond nibbles doggedly at my troubles and eventually bears them away. I love

Becky too much to be angry with her for long. As for the messed-up canvas, I'll turn it over and try again.

The human condition is a solipsistic monologue, punctuated with blurts and rebuttals. Catastrophe, like a high-decibel interruption, strikes when it is least expected. In the instances when it *is* expected, only a sage manages to inure himself or herself in the nick of time. Detachment, that most sought-after of attitudes, appears to be a chimera in our world of cradle-to-grave achievement. As we age, we compile our compendium of personal accomplishments like a police record. Felonies of material possession, frauds of self-importance. That's why, when I'm sitting at the pond, the tribulations of family and vocation melt into inconsequence. I'm witnessing the diametric opposite of a sitcom. The pond asserts itself as a refuge because it is a plain, equable place. The weeds at the water's edge form a wraparound bumper, an impact-absorber to cushion the jitters of the twentieth century, and the water (algae-free at the moment) is a smooth brown base upon which to construct quiet thoughts. Mentally and emotionally, I am rid of barriers. For once, I am not jumping hurdles. The reflection of the sky blots out the pain, the stupidity.

Then, I wish I were one of the dozen or so Israeli carp that loll just below the water's surface on sunny afternoons. Eight years ago, I stocked them as fingerlings; now, they're two feet, three feet long, timorous black submarines that, with a sudden sharp churning, disappear at the first intimation of danger. If I were like them, I, too, would duck out of harm's way. Instead, I manage to take life's roundhouses on the chin every time.

A pair of Canadian geese comes to the pond each spring. They set up a clamorous hegemony, building a nest of reeds at the water's edge. The mistress of the household sits on her eggs, head tucked under one wing, while the master assumes the role of guardian and protector. He paddles up and down the water's length, twisting his black neck and screwing his amber eye. When he notices my presence, he acts as if I am a usurper. *He* is the President of the Pond. To reinforce this notion, he does one of two things: either he commences a dreadful honking or he dismisses me entirely, pretending I'm not there. When the former turns into the latter, as it inevitably does, I feel his contempt. To a wild goose, I am nothing. My soothing blandishments and nonthreatening motions are but evidence that I am a useless creature. On the nest, his mate is perfectly safe. He goes about his business, plunging his head below the surface of the water in search of grub, only occasionally bothering to stare in my direction. I, of course, am the watcher of nature. I can't stop staring at him.

Sometimes on a warm afternoon in late April, before the goslings have hatched, I muster the courage to jump in. Father Goose is patrolling in his usual way, but he is not unmindful of my splash. A featherless biped, I am stunned by the chill. Gasping for breath and thrashing about to restore an equanimity of body temperature, I must present a clumsy spectacle to the master and mistress of flotation. Momentarily, Mother raises her head to give me the once over. Swimming laps in the long pond, I grant her nest a wide berth, curving my course so that I am close to the opposite bank. I don't want to cause any trouble. I know that wild geese have been known to attack humans on land; inviting an attack on water would be downright dangerous. I would be at a great disadvantage—a sitting duck. Father seems to sense my trepidation; he keeps his distance, but he reacts to my presence by maintaining a cautious escort, swimming ahead of me in one direction, then following from behind as I reverse course.

Later in summer, when the early segment of goose raising is over (soon after hatching, the goslings and their parents trek overland to a new habitat, so I lose track of them), I make a regular practice of swimming in the pond. Algae permitting, I swim ten or twelve laps and then I lie on the dock to let the sun dry me. The pond is my first line of defense against the sweltering inland Virginia heat. I have built four farm ponds in the last twenty years, primarily for this purpose (though occasionally I fish and canoe). I no longer own three of the ponds. This one, the latest and largest, will prove to be, I hope, a more permanent governance.

Finicky visitors don't share my natatory enthusiasm. "Y'all come over for a swim," I encourage them, but their half-hearted response makes me aware of the absurdity of my invitation. Generations have grown up equating aquatic exercise with tiled pools. If chemicals aren't up the nostrils and in the eyes, the water isn't clean enough. No matter how eager my guests might be for a cooling immersion, one glance at the murky depths (as well as a glance upstream at pasturing livestock) prompts that least sincere of excuses: "Maybe next time."

I can see the situation through their eyes. This thing I rhapsodize is just another farm pond—a watering hole, a widening of a stream, a mirror for bugs, a mecca for weeds. Its water goes rank during dry spells when inflow and outflow cease. It can smell like a methanous bog. It is home to snakes and snapping turtles. Insurance-wise, the pond is a liability, too—that's why No Trespassing signs are posted around it.

A decade ago, across the Blue Ridge in one of the earlier ponds, I was swimming the backstroke when I bumped hard against what felt like a floating two-by-four. It was a good-sized snapper, as surprised as I by our collision. In an instant, we both windmilled in opposite directions, equally shocked, equally unhinged, and I never swam the backstroke again in that pond without turning my head frequently to check for living obstructions.

I can relate other pond tales. The time the snake got in the canoe. The time the ecological balance was so out of kilter (before the pond was stocked) that biting water-skimmers chased me out of the water. The time poachers left frog carcasses—minus the legs—all over the place. The time an oil slick came downstream and fingerlings by the hundreds went belly up from lack of oxygen.

Farm ponds are river and bay and swamp rolled into one. The lacustrine layering of life is a delicate one, easily disturbed, and not necessarily a pretty sight. Between the microscope and the binoculars, creatures of every description parade into view. I go to the pond for the purpose of calming myself, but life as the pond inhabitants live it is anything but calm. A predatorial order prevails. Sometimes in the middle of a summer night, I will awaken to yelps of fright and agony, as one animal is finishing off another. The silent screams, of course, go unheeded—bug eating bug, fish eating fish. In every conceivable combination something is making a meal of something else. As President, I am out of the loop (if you don't count the mosquitoes and chiggers). When I'm at the pond, I am little more than a figurehead. I sit there, contented in my coarse grasp to find nothing amiss. The grass is mowed, the dead limbs are picked up, the muskrats are in check. My humanity keeps me at a remove from the drama that lurks below the surface of things here.

My family gets a kick out of my presidential self-appointment. They understand the pompousness of the title, which is really just a joke between us. They know that I've never been president of anything. I've managed to go through life without holding any elective office, and nobody has appointed me to high position either. Though I didn't consciously start out that way, I see now that I have avoided almost every opportunity to be a joiner, much less a leader, of any organization that would have had me.

By asserting myself as President of the Pond (despite Father Goose's seasonal objection), I am admitting that I may have missed a higher calling. I may have missed my chance to exert my influence over other people, to expand my few fields of expertise in such a way that I could have become an indispensable person in authority. But it is probably too late now, and I really don't mind. I have been busy. Preserving the creative person at the core of my being has been a full-time occupation. Like a dragonfly, I have flitted across many surfaces in search of the perfect expression. The pond job was up for grabs, so I took it. Whichever way birds, beasts, fish, and insects interpret me, and whatever my wife and children may think, I'm just a man sitting in a chair, trying to distill the fundamental beauty from a nondescript body of water.

SIX

T HE YEAR I STARTED SECOND GRADE, my parents' bucolic
fascination reached its apogee and they bought a house and twenty-
seven acres in West Kingston that belonged to a colleague of my father's
at the University of Rhode Island. Despite its improvements, our house
in Kingston—where we had lived for three years—was tight quarters for
a growing family of five. Moreover, my father found the location oppressive, situated as it was at the foot of the campus, within sight and
earshot of everything he wanted to get away from at the end of a day.

The property in West Kingston lay a quarter of a mile back from the
paved road in an area that was mostly scrub woods and overgrown
fields. It included an abandoned sand pit and cranberry bog on either
side of a trout-filled stream. The house was a split-gable, two-story,
crudely carpentered structure that sat within a loop of driveway on a
cedar-dotted rise criss-crossed with ancient stone fences along an abandoned wagon road that was the former hypotenuse of two intersecting
byways, Waites Corner Road and South County Trail. The house's
dominant features were a blocky central fireplace and chimney of glacial
boulders (known as "fieldstones"), and a front porch smothered in rambling rosebushes. To one side was a pyramid-roofed outbuilding com-
prising a shallow garage (it fitted a Model T, so the rump of our 1950s
family sedan always stuck out) and a three-windowed storage room that
became my father's studio. A chicken coop stood nearby, in which we
found glass eggs—placebos to keep the laying hens in production. At one
corner of the yard was an outdoor grill of fieldstone; its cooking surface
was an inch-thick slab of armor plate that undoubtedly originated at the
naval base at Quonset Point. The outflung branches of a centenary oak,
with a couple of swings suspended, shaded a picnic table.

From the viewpoint of a seven-year-old, the new property was an
uncharted challenge. I busied myself in all directions—exploring the

woods, claiming a camp beneath a particular white pine (my parents let me sleep overnight there in an old tent most of the summer), building forts and tree houses, wading in the creek (and picking leeches off my legs when I got out). I raced my bicycle along the sandy lane, plashing vee's of water as I bisected puddles. Poking around the sand pit, a habitat for rattlesnakes that had been defiled by decades of trash dumping, I had an entrepreneurial brainstorm: I'd manufacture sandpaper. The chicken coop would be my factory. With the help of my sister and brother, I organized a bucket brigade to bring the raw material up from the sand pit (an event I'll always remember because I came within inches of stepping on a sunning rattler). We used sheets of my mother's best typing paper and a bottle of mucilage to make the prototypes. Needless to say, there was a lot of leftover sand. In our spare time, we fashioned miniature canoes from the ghostly peelings of birch.

With his redoubtable energy and impracticality, my father initiated the improvements he thought were necessary for the twenty-seven acres. The first thing he did was move the outhouse from our previous property. A functioning two-holer with a determinedly contemporary stench, it was a rugged, cedar-shingled affair (with a star cutout centered on its door) that did not readily part company with its underpinnings. With the aid of four able-bodied students, he managed to tip the topmost third of the privy into the trunk of a borrowed coupé. Boards were jammed underneath for support, then ropes were tied every which way, trussing the load so it wouldn't fall off. I remember riding in the car that followed, and being consumed with excitement as I witnessed the slow progression of the two black holes en route to West Kingston. I wanted to be first user! The outhouse was conveyed three miles to its new location, beyond the farthermost corner of the backyard, next to a stone fence wreathed in poison ivy. Naturally, my father hadn't thought about digging a pit beforehand, so when we got there, correcting this nagging oversight took the rest of the afternoon. I was forced to relieve myself in the woods.

Actually, my father's single-mindedness in relocating the outhouse *was* rooted in a practical notion: it would save wear and tear on the house plumbing, not to mention reducing our water consumption. (The shallow well was prone to running dry, and there was no septic system to speak of, just a malodorous cesspool down the hill, where day lilies grew twice as tall as anywhere else.) My father figured that with so much land of our own, we'd be spending plenty of time outdoors, and he was right to a certain extent. A privy in a central place on the property was the logical place to heed the calls of nature. What he didn't take into account, though, was the environment of the outhouse itself—that darkly claustrophobic locus of mud-daubers, that nostril-shocker of dried fecal matter and quicklime. He overestimated its attractiveness as a place of convenience.

Like good children, we made frequent use of the newly installed facility. But once the novelty wore off, my brother and sister and I, and our friends, found it much more enjoyable to evacuate our bowels in plein air. We relished the uninhibited freedom of pulling down our pants in the great outdoors and choosing large and interesting leaves—anything but poison ivy—instead of the humdrum squares on the roll. Besides, the instant appreciation of the blue flies that iridescently decorated our droppings made our efforts doubly rewarding. As children are wont to do, we made a competition of it—counting the flies, comparing the physical nuances of our evacuations. We chose an area behind the garage, between it and the old wagon trail, for our defecation grounds. In the course of that first summer, we turned the overgrown meadow of wild blueberries and wild cherries into a minefield of shit. *We* were careful where we stepped, but inevitably the day came when my father, in one of his fits of proprietary rectitude, came crashing through with his hand-pumped poison ivy sprayer. After the comedy of his sole-scraping pirouettes of disgust, we were spanked royally. Remanded to the outhouse, we went to the bathroom indoors, more or less, after that.

The outhouse became instead a laboratory for sexual discovery. Having watched our mixed beagle, Polly, mate with Raffles, the scottie that belonged to our nearest neighbor, my sister and her best friend, and my brother and I and *our* friends decided it was time for a closer inspection of each others' private parts. These self-taught sex education sessions took place behind the latched door with its five-pointed fixed spotlight. It was all very interesting, playing doctor in the crowded privy, but it generated more questions than any of us were knowledgeable enough to answer. Looking back, it amazes me that neither of my parents ever heard our giggles.

I went to second and third grades at the West Kingston school, about a mile away, a T-shaped three-room schoolhouse across from the railroad tracks. Second and fourth grade fronted the building; third grade was to the rear toward the playground. Three grades, three rooms, three years—the simplicity of the sequence made me feel secure. I'd start off on the left, move to the back, and finish up on the right. It was a school I would flourish in because things were so spelled out. Monday through

Friday, by bicycle or on foot, I took a shortcut through a neighbor's woods. At one place I had to cross a single plank bridge over a creek (a breath-holding feat of navigation on a bike). Along the way I'd stop to pick blueberries and skip stones in the water, or whittle sticks with my penknife and chase rabbits into the underbrush. The kids riding the school bus envied me for my twice-daily ramble through the country-side, so I'd frequently enjoin friends to walk home with me. The accompanied peregrination took a leisurely hour or more, and there was always a logistical problem when suppertime came—someone had to drive my visitors home.

As much as I was learning in school, I got a parallel education on the twenty-seven acres. There was no corner of the property I left unexamined. As I roamed, I compiled practical knowledge: how to use a hand-saw, how to hammer a nail, how to fish, how to identify animal tracks. Finding a discarded hatchet, I taught myself the art of chopping down trees. For a while nothing pleased me more than wielding my hatchet; I envisioned clearing land on a grand scale, my specialty being cedars. At one point, I laid low a prominent cedar near the edge of the yard, a tree my father was partial to for its symmetry and size. The disciplinary tempest I weathered only sent me into deeper territory.

In the old cranberry-harvesting days, the stream on the property had been dammed down the hill from our house, resulting in a placid crook in one meander. I decided to build a boat. In the basement, I found the perfect flotation devices, two wooden packing crates that had contained my parents' record collection (breakable 78s) during their many moves. After promising that the crates could be reverted to their original use whenever necessary—although it pained me to think that we might move again—I took a putty knife and applied the contents of a can of roofing tar to their cracks and joints. Lo! I had two watertight, if some-what sticky, pontoons. I placed a board athwart the boxes for a seat and fashioned an oar from a bean pole and a wooden shingle. Getting in the boat was tricky, for it was eminently capsizable, bobbing as it did in three pieces. With care, I'd arrange myself—a foot in each box, my seated weight on the board holding them together—all the while steadying myself with the oar against the skunk cabbage bank. Underway, the going was more stable, even serene, as long as I made no sudden moves. I christened the craft *Lazy River*, a name I thought to be so original that I lettered it on the sides of the crates with a brush and a tube of alizarin crimson from my father's paintbox.

I learned how to use our Toro, the rotary power mower my father acquired when he realized that his push-type reel mower wasn't sufficient for the grooming of an "estate," as my mother called it. By to-day's standards, the Toro was primitive—a heavy, vibrating, hard-to-push machine with a temperamental one-and-one-half horsepower gas engine that started with many pulls of a rope painstakingly wrapped around a notched spindle. (The pull that coaxed the engine to life was always one pull short of arm-wrenching defeat.) My father knew noth-ing about the maintenance of a power mower; it never occurred to him to change the oil or sharpen the blade. He left it to me to fiddle with the thing, so with an inspired ignorance I did what I could. I'd clean the spark plug, re-set the fuel and air mixture screws on the carburetor, fill the gas tank, top off the crankcase, scrape at the gouges on the blade with an old scythe stone, and somehow the Toro limped along. My adjust-ments were by ear and by eye; after a couple years of these ministrations, it was a wonder that the machine ran at all.

But mowing with the Toro was an infinitely enriching experience. It was the next best thing to driving a car, I imagined. I could roar a twenty-four-inch path to the outhouse and back. I could tame unruly weeds. I could bump the mower against the trunks of the ubiquitous ce-dars, creating archipelagos in our acreage that were parklike, picnic-ready. Over time, my father and I extended the boundaries of the lawn across the road and down to the stream. True, the mower's wheels were bolted in their highest position, so that even after we mowed, the ground was riddled with tufts, chewed stumps, supine briars, and blade-glanced rocks. Besides, I was too short to exert much force against the handlebar. Mowing downhill was easy, but mowing uphill took deter-mination. Doggedly, I pretended I was a human tractor.

I breezed through second and third grade, earning enthusiastic enco-miums from my teachers, Mrs. Smith and Miss Kenyon. With my con-fidence at an all-time high, every classmate was my friend. A photograph taken at my eighth birthday party shows me as the center of attention, the dispenser of goodwill and justice. I'm making sure everyone is having a rip-roaring time, I'm encouraging universal participation in the party games.

Yes, I was a ringleader, but a kindly, egalitarian one. My goal was to encourage everyone to learn the things I had learned (but only if they wanted to). I could be counted upon to organize, to insist on fair play, to keep score. In the school yard at West Kingston, I excelled at dodge-ball and tag. I shinnied up the galvanized supports of the swing sets. I butt-bumped and butt-jumped on the see-saw. I whirled like crazy on

49

the push-and-pull merry-go-round (a playground addition that was considered dangerous and eventually dismantled). I out-shouted my friends in the meaningless, mind-numbing chant, *I like Ike, I like Ike* . . .

The projects I undertook during the summer months corroborated the blossoming of my self-assurance. I ranged farther into the woods than ever before, blazing new trails with my hatchet, which rarely found repose in its belt-hung sheath. I constructed deer feeding stations—low platforms of logs and branches on which I piled meadow grass. (By winter, I realized the absurdity of this notion, for when I tramped through the snow to check on them, no animal had so much as touched a stem of my wild hay.) I made bows and arrows, spears, slingshots, fishing poles. I built an armada of warships from wood scraps. I climbed every tree worth climbing. On an expedition far upstream, I discovered a broader, unrippled stretch of water, a true Lazy River. By the end of summer vacation, I had drawn a map on a paper garment bag from the drycleaners—a guide to our twenty-seven acres, crammed with new-found detail, utilizing every color in the crayon box.

When the fall term began, I entered the rightmost classroom of West Kingston school—Mrs. Hudson's finally attainable fourth grade—but I stayed there only one day. My mother had made up her mind that I should skip fourth grade. She had been dropping hints all summer long, asking me if school seemed too easy, inquiring as to how I'd feel if I were to part company with my classmates. Then, in the face of my ambivalent answers, she'd blast me with her adult, authoritative opinion: I wasn't being challenged sufficiently, I was too old for my grade, I needed to take school more seriously. Her grillings confused me. I thought I had been doing well in school. Academic perfection was my goal, and I achieved it handily. Memorizing the multiplication tables, matching up the names and places in geography, aping the meticulous, slanted penmanship in the Palmer folder—I applied myself and did everything right. I even enjoyed schoolwork. Wasn't that all that could be expected of me?

I had heard about kids skipping grades, but it had never happened to anyone I knew. Grade-skippers were super-smart. Anyone would be flattered to belong in such a category, but I was sure that I didn't. Yet as my third-grade summer dwindled to Labor Day weekend, I was directly propositioned about the possibility of going straight to fifth grade, which was back at Kingston in the old grammar school. Hesitatingly, I gave my assent. It was my mother's wish, so I figured it would be advantageous for me. And so the second day of school, without goodbyes or transitional ceremony of any kind, I was on a schoolbus full of jabbering strangers, heading for a destiny that would dog me throughout the remaining years of my schooling: being the youngest kid in class.

As an instant fifth grader, I was smaller than the other kids, too. Minutes after I arrived in the strange classroom, the school custodian came by with an adjustable wrench to lower the seat and desktop of my unitary steel-and-wood desk. The tittering accompaniment on all four sides made me feel smaller still. I was a midget, physically and intellectually. The teacher, Miss King, had obviously accepted me against her better judgment, for she gave me no preferential treatment, not even during those first moments. After introducing me to the class, explaining that I had come directly from third grade (unappreciative guffaws, a mock groan or two), she put me in the regular rotation—to be called on just like anybody else. But my answers were almost always wrong. I didn't know the capital of Montana. I couldn't spell Mississippi. The problems in long division I attempted to solve at the blackboard terminated in chalk dust and error. Miss King was dispassionate as to whether I sank or swam; my staying in her class would hinge on my own fortitude. She was not one for coddling.

To the amusement of my peers, I raised my hand so many times to go to the boys' room I was denied the privilege altogether. I developed a stammer. Recovering from a succession of colds, I sniffled into Kleenex by the boxful, and instead of disposing of them, I stuffed them in my desk. One day in her post-class prowling, Miss King opened my desktop, only to discover my sizable cache of expended tissue. She was aghast. My parents were summoned to an emergency *tête-à-tête*, at which they were shown the incriminating deskful and asked what should be done, i.e., wasn't it time for me to go back to fourth grade where I rightfully belonged? My father said he didn't think so, and he took it upon himself to dispose of the evidence. He urged her to bear with me. (When he got home, he lectured me sternly about the need to throw away Kleenex as I used them.) The following morning, I noticed with relief that the offending contents of my desk half-filled the wire wastebasket next to Miss King's desk.

At home, not many weeks later, I was careless with the hatchet and almost killed myself as a result. I had just felled a good-sized cedar, but sinews of heartwood still joined the crown to the stump. I began using the blunt end of the hatchet to bludgeon the tree apart. Raising the hatchet over my head in a windup for a mighty blow, I put the blade right through my hat, slicing the skin on top of my head, very nearly splitting my skull. I didn't know what I had done until, my task finished, I wiped my brow and discovered that my fingers were smeared with blood. A fast ride to the emergency room at the South County Hospital, a shaved spot in my proudly combed head of hair, a dozen stitches, and a bandage that looked like one of my mother's sanitary pads sobered me to the perils of my long-standing pastime. The imperative to chop down cedars suddenly lost its urgency.

One afternoon, during the day or two I recuperated from my self-inflicted wound, a marvelous thing happened: my father came home early from the university and spent a couple of hours playing with me on the floor of my room. He had never done this before (and would never do it again). Whether his motivation was one of guilt, or concern, or just plain relief after a son's close call, I'll never know. He was down beside me most of the afternoon, helping me build cities with blocks, pushing my diecast toy vehicles around roads on the rug pattern, landing my airplanes on runways delineated by the floorboards, galloping my plastic horses and their bowlegged cowboys and Indians in imaginary assaults and missions of mercy. We were sharing a fantasy. I was transported with happiness, and he seemed to be enjoying himself, too.

Somehow those few hours of my father's undivided attention gave me the courage to face the slings and arrows of fifth grade. I was stumbling as never before, losing ground as fast as I gained it, and yet I could already see that this was the way of the real world. The easy path was over, and over for good, but I would have reached its end sooner or later. By admitting failure into my childish expectations, I was becoming a stronger person. So this was what they meant when they patted you on the head and said, "You're really growing up!"

Two additional factors helped me overcome my handicaps in Miss King's class—a girl and a snare drum. The girl was Adah Cummins, the only child of an English professor at the university. She sat across the aisle from me, poised and posture-perfect with her back squarely against the seat, and when she walked, she walked with a regal carriage. To me she was Guinevere—an aloof beauty with long honey tresses, a mouth pursed in thought, and green eyes that cast unhurried glances in my direction before returning to some inner recollection. A year older than I, she was a straight-A student who never gave a wrong answer. She took private art lessons in Kingston two days a week after school. She played clarinet in the school band. I loved her with a dignified, Arthurian adoration. Being so talented and beautiful, she deserved nothing less (though

I couldn't help but notice that she wasn't popular with her classmates, most of whom thought she was stuck up).

To be near Adah and worthy of her attention, I realized it was necessary to emulate her. I applied myself a little more strenuously to my homework assignments. I lobbied my parents to enroll me in the same art class, which they did. And I joined the school band that practiced in the school basement, ostensibly to play clarinet.

But another clarinetist was not needed. My sister, a grade ahead of me, was already in the band playing glockenspiel, so the band director, a Mr. Bruno Houdlin—whose name, manner, and origins caused hilarious speculation on the part of his musicians—steered me in the direction of the snare drum. The Svenson kids were good at percussion. Memories of nursery school rhythm band came flooding back as I learned to distinguish between flams and rolls, between sixteenths, eighths, quarters, halfs, and wholes. I drummed with joy, with abandon (Mr. Houdlin's effeminate hands often gesturing me to trim the volume). It felt so good to be thrumming the backbone of a march while Adah's tootling clarinet carried the melody.

My zealousness must have disrupted the equilibrium of the ensemble, for later in the year a clarinet position came open and Mr. Houdlin put me in it. The switch didn't bother me in the least, for now I could sit beside my beloved Adah. Of course, I played a second (or third) clarinet to her first, and the school instrument I used was a one-piece, sour-tasting, nickel-plated version of her lovely silver-and-ebony instrument, which disassembled into five precious sections that fitted into blue plush depressions within a leatherette case. But it didn't matter that I started playing from scratch, or that every other sound from the bell of my clarinet was a squeak or a squeal. It didn't matter that I was a displaced drummer boy whose mouth ached with the strain of unexpected employment as I bit down on the bakelite mouthpiece and its tickling reed. What mattered was that Adah and I were harmonizing. On occasion, Mr. Houdlin even gave us private instruction together. As we sat there, she and I, beneath the spreading ductwork of the coal-fired furnace, thoughts of wild love filled me that found only halting expression in the notes that belabored my lungs, tongue, and fingertips. Our duets were fusions of the rough and the smooth, edgy with the *frisson* of boy versus girl, and all the while delineated in space by Mr. Houdlin's ever-watchful fingers.

I can't say that Adah opened her heart to me and loved me the way I loved her, but we became friends. I never spoke to her about my love for her—I was far too shy. She may not have even guessed that I loved her at all. Then again, she may not have wanted my love. I do know that she valued my friendship because she told me so. If anything characterized our relationship, it was *seriousness*. We had serious conversations, and we studied music and art together seriously. As we walked beneath the elms on the way to our after-school art lesson, she exerted a calming influence on me, a feeling I still preserve from the trauma of that year. She made me feel grown up.

SEVEN

The Oliver 550 becomes the mainstay of my haymaking operation because of its superior weight and power. Farming neighbors who see me working in the field ask, "How's the little Oliver running?" They recall that the 550 was the smallest tractor in the Oliver line at the time of its manufacture. It isn't so little to me, but I can't tell them that. These guys operate really beefy tractors, ones with ladders and air conditioners. I wonder what they thought when I was farming with just the Kubota? Hell, I know what they thought. They thought I was nuts.

My old field mower, or cutter bar, is an Oliver, too. According to the 550's instruction manual, which has been preserved in the tractor's toolbox, tractor and mower are factory-matched, but my "new" tractor is never hitched to the Oliver mower. I *trade up*, as farmers say, to a mower-conditioner.

A mower-conditioner is an improvement, or rather an enlargement upon a standard field mower, for it includes a reel in front that pushes the crop into the cutter bar (to cut the crop more efficiently) and a pair of rollers in back that crush, or "condition" the mown material as it passes to the rear (to promote faster drying). My purchase, a New Holland 474 Haybine, is a mower-conditioner that has been used for only one season, although it looks much older. An accidental acid overspray has severely blistered its paint; no longer red and yellow in the familiar New Holland two-tone, it looks as if a barn burned to the ground around it. Trucked down from a consignment auction in Pennsylvania by a local farmer who dabbles in equipment sales, the machine is priced to sell. At a third of its ten-thousand-dollar list price, it costs me as much as all the other implements together, including the tractor.

Yet I was strongly motivated to make the trade. On a final cutting of the previous season, four days of drying (the usual length of time to wait before raking and baling) resulted in the loss of the crop. The first three days were sunny and the grass dried splendidly, but on the fourth day it began to rain. It rained for a week. There was no way the hay could be saved. If it had been cut with a mower-conditioner, I could have raked and baled on the second day, and gotten the bales into the barn before noontime on the third. An "if" like that exasperates me no end; in this case, five hundred dollars rotted away to mulch on the unraked field. Much as I enjoy using the old Oliver mower, and labor diligently over its field-readiness (keeping its reciprocating knives sharp, attending to its lubrication), I realize the necessity for parting with it.

A good used mower-conditioner is not easy to find. I feel fortunate having located the 474, which is New Holland's top-of-the-line Haybine with a seven-foot cut. The seller lets me pay in installments as hay is sold. Cash for the downpayment comes from a Mennonite farmer, who has conveniently turned up to purchase the Oliver mower. A practitioner from the old school—porkpie-hatted, nearing seventy—he chooses to stay with the tried and true. He doesn't believe in conditioned hay—his cows don't take to it, he says. God gave cows teeth and the Devil gave man newfangled machinery. I help him load the old mower onto his truck, and he drives off into the sunset while I await the dawning of the state-of-the-art.

The 474 is a hefty piece of equipment, even larger than my baler, and like the baler, it incorporates diverse mechanisms that are powered by the drive shaft from the PTO. Its spring-tined reel, rotating at two and a half times the speed of its ground wheels, pushes the standing crop into the knives. To the rear, the spinning rolls, like wringers with raised hard-rubber chevrons, crush the cut material as it is flung through. An adjustable baffle behind the rolls governs the width of the swath. Some mower-conditioners' mechanisms are connected by serpentine belts, others are connected by roller chains; likewise, some are as jointed as marionettes, and others are straight-shafted. In some mower-conditioners, the reciprocating knives are propelled by a pitman arm, while others utilize a device called a wobble joint. Some have multiple transmissions, others have a single transmission that turns a hookup of whirling complexity. The New Holland 474 has three transmissions, two belts, one chain, one wobble joint, and nine universal joints.

The implement is towed from a swinging tongue that offsets the whole machine to the right of the tractor during the mowing operation. It is adjusted for height hydraulically. A remote valve beside the tractor seat controls the ten-foot-wide, three-thousand-pound implement by means of two high-pressure hoses that run along the tongue and over the top of the roll housing to a hydraulic cylinder.

A mower-conditioner can be operated at a faster ground speed than a field mower, a qualification that enhances its desirability as a time saver. After the crop is rammed through the knives and rolls, it is deposited in a loosely layered swath, stems spread perpendicularly to the direction of travel. Depending on the type of crop and its density, the rolls can be adjusted for pinch pressure by means of a torsion bar.

If mower-conditioners have one drawback, aside from their price, it is the noise they make. The voluminous sheet-metal enclosure of the 474 amplifies the clanking of its separately sprung header (the reel plus knife assembly) as well as the clatter of its wobble drive and rolls. Every bump and jolt translates into sound, the sum of it deafening. When a slug of thick material passes between the rolls, the hullabaloo can be frightening. Mowing in the field now, I learn to ignore sonic transients. My neighbors horrify me with stories of groundhogs and raccoons, even cats and dogs, accidentally crushed with a terrified yawp above the din before their flattened, mangled bodies are flung out to dry. Farmers take pride in the inexorability of their mower-conditioners.

I soon get in the habit of wearing headphone-style hearing protectors. Although the Oliver 550 is a quiet tractor, quieter than the Kubota, the mower-conditioner racket exceeds my threshold of pain (the noise of the baler is a close second). Hearing protectors take some getting used to; the spring pressing the anechoic muffs over my ears is like a vise clamping my skull. Wearing them for extended periods makes my head sweat and ache, especially when I've got sunglasses on. But by isolating myself in a cocoon of auditory dullness, I can concentrate on straighter rows and cleaner turns. I can more fully appreciate the music of the thrumming machinery, which, contextually, isn't much different from the music of the spheres. It's a ringing-humming that rocks the soul, a lullaby of larger themes. At times, I even imagine a singsong voice making a gentle mockery of me as I work:

What farmer do I know
Arrives at an equipment plateau?

Usually it's a sign that I've been out in the field too long when I start to hear such things. But the imagined couplet contains a simple truth: the acquired paraphernalia of haymaking becomes an open-ended wish list, as the haymaker can afford it. I buy a welding unit to make my own repairs. I buy a generator for the barn. I stock baling twine, replacement

knives, replacement tines, shear pins. And not many months later, I am
the inevitable owner of a twenty-four-foot skeleton hay elevator, which
is a ladderlike, portable conveyer for square bales. Stacking and unstack-
ing bales by the hundreds within the recesses of the big barn *should* require some form of mechanical assistance. I am a logical acquisitor – my
back takes precedent over my wallet.

The elevator is "skeleton" because its hoisting chain travels in an open
tubular frame, as opposed to a hay and grain elevator, in which the chain
is encased in a sheet-metal trough. Powered by an electric motor, the
contraption moves bales either horizontally or on an incline up to forty-
five degrees. It is a labor saver of epic usefulness when transporting bales
to and from the upper reaches of a full mow.

Yet few farmers use hay elevators anymore, now that most forage
crops are round baled or chopped into ensilage (fodder that will undergo
anaerobic acid fermentation in the silo). New skeleton elevators bear
absurd price tags. A used elevator will rarely surface at an equipment dispersal auction; I hadn't seen one in months. I placed a week-long adver-
tisement in the newspaper classifieds with no response. I ran the ad a
second week, and the day after it expired, I chased down a solitary offer.
A local farmer was going out of business – the perennial denouement.
He and his wife showed me an ancient Snowco elevator that looked as
if it had been dropped from a high place. Its motor ran the chain backward unless its drive belt was twisted into a figure eight. More than one
coat hanger had been utilized to hold cracked welds together.

"She runs, don't she, hon?" the farmer announced for my benefit,
delegating to his wife the responsibility of plugging in the frayed and
cobwebbed cord. Miraculously, she wasn't electrocuted. The forsaken
implement sprang to life.

"How much?" I asked, wary to be asking at all, but considering, too,
the rarity of the item. I was at a disadvantage; he could ask (and get) any
price that popped into his head.

"Oh, fifty bucks," he replied.

We carried the elevator to the pickup. It was heavy and its rust came
off on our hands. We secured it with baling twine at a balancing point
between the tailgate and the roof of the cab, where, like an airframe,
its extremities extended beyond the front and rear bumpers. A more un-
gainly, decrepit load I couldn't imagine. The scrap yard was its rightful
destination. I began to mourn the loss of fifty hard-earned dollars.

But some welding, some adjustment, and a few replacement parts
bring the elevator back into service. And it really does make the barn-

work easier. Once again, I've added a resurrected piece of equipment to the fold, yet in doing so, I cross a rubicon of sorts. As far as haymaking is concerned, my equipment-buying days are over. Suppressing the lust for bigger and better, there is nothing else I need. The rest is up to me: good judgment, safe operation, regular maintenance, and a commitment to long hours in the field.

By my fourth season of haymaking, I have added a couple of improvements to the regimen, which enable me to work less rigorously. While I mow and bale with the Oliver, I rake and pull the wagon with the Kubota. That way, I can have one tractor hitched up and ready to roll as I finish with the other. I save time this way – hitching and unhitching, fueling and lubricating when the workday is over. Also, I'm dividing the long field hours between two aging machines.

In obedience to the imperative to make hay while the sun shines, I've rigged up a parasol for use on either tractor out of an old golf umbrella and a length of pipe bolted to one fender. Despite the straw hat, long sleeves, gloves, sunglasses, and sunscreen lotion, I need more protection from the sun. A barrier of shade, however slight, is conducive to alertness and attention. Straying off the row, lowering a wheel into a groundhog hole, clogging a mechanism, breaking a knife – calamity befalls me now and then, but if I react to it with a cool head, I can analyze the problem and solve it quicker.

The degree or two less heat and the footcandle or two less glare under the parasol also gives me the chance to decouple my brain periodically from the seemingly endless spiral. Midway through a field, time tends to drag. If I am relatively comfortable and unfazed – and not trying to beat a nasty turn of weather – I can stop the tractor, climb off, take a break.

I am mindful of the fact that farming continues to top the list of hazardous occupations. Ironically, the more advanced the machinery, the more susceptible the farmer is to injury. There is no easy way to farm. The best course of action is to reduce as many affronts to human dignity as possible. To try, but not monomaniacally; to work, but not like a dog. At the start, I wanted to jump in and do it all by myself, and that was a mistake. When I realized my labor alone was inadequate for the most physically demanding part of haymaking – picking up the bales from the fields – I grasped at the nearest solution by soliciting the aid of Becky, Van, and Hope. But these are not the days of family-powered farms. The hay is *my* thing. With the children gone most of the time now, and with Becky busy as ever with her teaching, I'm on my own. It's up to me to find a willing labor pool.

So I photocopy a poster extolling the virtues of haymaking on the Cross Keys battlefield, and tack it to the bulletin boards at James Madison University and Becky's office door. In block letters I enumerate the benefits: sunshine, exercise, camaraderie, pay well above minimum wage, and, yes, history. The response is immediate, the phone rings day and night. I swiftly compile a list of students who'll come over on short notice. They're not only eager to lift bales, they're begging to lift bales.

And in practice, student labor is an ideal solution. For my young helpers, it's a temporary, fresh-air alternative to a humdrum, part-time gig such as babysitting or delivering pizzas. In turn, I am blessed with the muscle power necessary to get the hay into the barn quickly. Kubota-drawn and on foot, we roam the crewcut fields with the haywagon, tossing aboard the cubic compactions one by one, and when the wagon is tottering full, my helpers sit on top of the load while I navigate the tractor toward the barn. I suspect they'll never have a more meaningful or satisfying hayride.

A session of bale collecting usually ends by dinnertime. Loading and stacking three, four consecutive wagonloads reduces the lot of us to the same sweat-drenched, hay-bedecked common denominator. We are itching and sneezing and sharing a ragged chorus of complaints that is constantly undermined by laughter. From time to time, I regale my co-workers with tidbits about the Civil War battle.

"You mean this was where those dudes fought? Right here?"

"Yup. Right here." And heaving a bale to the fourth tier on the wagon, I'll recount some detail or statistic. My words may go in one ear and out the other, but they're not wasted. Most likely, they'll crop up again during later, cooler moments – in a textbook, on a TV program. Breath thus expended conforms to the balance scale of Newtonian physics, and preservation of the lesson is assured. To work up a sweat under a burning late-morning sun is as good a way as any to enter and exit history. My helpers will never forget the making of hay at Cross Keys, this I do not doubt.

EIGHT

In 1954, the summer I finished fifth grade, our family was uprooted again—this time to New York City. For several years, my father had been taking post-graduate courses in business administration at MIT, riding the train from Kingston to Boston and back one day a week, and now he was determined to go ahead and finish his doctorate—a preliminary to getting a better-paying teaching position than the one he held at the University of Rhode Island.

Having been granted a year's leave of absence without pay, he enrolled himself in New York University as a full-time doctoral candidate in management, studying under such preeminent authorities as Lillian Gilbreth and Peter Drucker. For my father, it was a refreshing break from the insularity of "Li'l Rhody." The ambience of Wall Street, the interaction with young professionals from the largest corporations in America, and the opportunity to take up a serious learning regimen wrought noticeable changes in him. I rarely saw my father anymore, and when I did, he was detached from day-to-day events, as if he were a visitor to our household. My world as a fifth grader became unduly ephemeral. During the last month of school, I went through the motions—waking up, surviving in the classroom, coming home, doing homework, going to bed—without feeling as if I was really there. Consequently, I don't remember much of this period. My father's lack of interest made our lives seem uninteresting to us.

Our family must have left Rhode Island in a great hurry, for my memory is vague about everything except the drive southward along the Merritt Parkway, during which I took note of the differing architecture of the overpasses. As one of three bickering siblings in the back seat, I was contributing to the general anxiety. The wind rushing in the windows partially drowned out our irate vocalizing but exacerbated the tension. When my father finally yelled at us to shut up, my mother ventured into the sullen void by recounting vignettes from her Manhattan childhood, back in the days when horse-drawn livery clattered outside the family residence on 109th Street. Her voice had a way of disarming the on-going rivalry in the back seat. Calmer now, we totted the miles. My father's freckled hands, his right one tendering a burning cigarette, played the top half of the steering wheel as I listened respectfully to the prematurely graying wave at the back of my mother's head. In arrhythmical slappings, the family sedan bucketed across the expansion joints, slipping past the populous outskirts of lower Connecticut, then entering still more crowded environs with names that sounded like animal noises: Yonkers, the Bronx.

I had been to New York City twice before on Christmas holidays, so I thought I knew what to expect. Both times we had encamped for a long weekend in an inexpensive midtown hotel, the Schuyler, a repository of burnished elevators, ill-lit corridors, and windows that opened onto sunless airshafts. With my brother and sister and me in tow, my mother had revisited the places that were familiar to her: the window-dressed emporiums along Fifth Avenue, the thoroughfares of Central Park, the touristic skyscrapers, the monuments to genius and valor at prominent intersections. Everywhere we walked, storefronts made me giddy with yuletide covetousness; I wished I had the fine apparel, the wristwatches, the ship models, the electric trains.

But this time our destination was not B. Altman's, or Lord & Taylor's, or F.A.O. Schwartz, or the Wollman Rink, or Rockefeller Center. My father drove straight to 118th Street and Morningside Park, where a furnished apartment on a summer's lease awaited us. This was the residence of the Farriés (friends of my great aunt), who were vacationing in Europe. Their apartment was on the top floor of a well-maintained building at the extremity of respectable—i.e., Caucasian—Morningside Heights. In every room were paintings that featured nymphs and fauns, or a heap of fruit on a tabletop, and most of the gilt frames had little lamps attached that weakly illuminated the umber scenes. Ornate, highly polished furniture commandeered corners, and there were oriental rugs, and drapes that hushed the sun and the street. At one end of the living room stood a Steinway parlor grand, shawl-bedecked, with turned ebony legs that themselves were icons of contemplation.

Not having actually met the Farriés, I learned they were an idealized family of four: he a professor at Columbia, she an accomplished pianist, a daughter enrolled at a women's college of excellence in Massachusetts, a son at one of the local prep schools prefixed with "Saint." I moved among their belongings with reverence, breathing a rarefied air and absorbing the haute style and flair. Usually the Farriés summered in Canada at a place called Cache Lake, and an acquaintance of Mrs. Farrié had written and illustrated a book about it that was left lying around. Conveniently, it became my favorite book; I vowed to write one day my own pastoral idyll, and execute my own beguiling pen-and-ink chapter headings. I vowed, too, to become a model plane builder like the son, whose handiwork hung by thumbtack and thread from the ceiling of his bedroom.

On the Farriés' Steinway I initiated my lifelong romance with the piano. The way it growled or tittered at its opposite ivory poles beckoned my unskilled fingers. Not only was the instrument a ready interpolator of my innate, though ignorant ear, it was invitingly easy to make music on. Pumping its pedals was like driving a car. With no prior training, I navigated the simpler selections stored within the hinged bench seat, selections the Farrié children must have practiced and passed beyond aeons ago. Middle C was my lodestar. With my father's help, I was able to make sense of the finger numbering system, a perturbing logic that challenged me to render simultaneously both treble and bass clefs. My most advanced accomplishment of the summer was Haydn's "Happy Farmer," which I dexterously honed from a stop-and-go jog to a breakneck, *sempre forte* dash.

I loved that damn tune so much I hummed it wherever I went. I was the happiest farmer in Manhattan—the rube from Rhode Island. The city's sidewalks and subways revealed the infinite shadings of humanity, multipurposeful and bewildering in variety. The spectrum of people astonished me. I could see that my upbringing had been provincial, to say the least. West Kingston was comfortable like an old coat, but now I was in the clothing store, confronting the racks of possibilities. My imagination became fortified as never before. To confront so many races, physiques, and languages all at once made me feel like an explorer. To a ten-year-old fresh from the certitudes of small-town New England, the stimulation was as if I had been dropped off the edge of the world. My mind was so absorbed that I sometimes walked into things: lampposts, fire hydrants, passersby. If my mother hadn't been there to lead me around during those first few weeks in the city, I would have wandered off on a stumbling tangent of amazement, happily humming Haydn.

I loved the Museum of Natural History, its Rooseveltian rectitude that spoke to every American boy. I loved the brown elephants and the zeppelin whale. I wished I could walk right through the plate glass into the dioramas, for their stunning rectangles of floodlight and taxidermy in the darkened hall seemed more real than life itself. True, I had migrated from twenty-seven real acres in Rhode Island, but here were North America, Africa, Asia, Australia, and Antarctica all in a row, one jewel case after another, each awaiting an unhurried inspection, and the birds, the beasts all stood still.

My mother took us to Riverside Park and Grant's Tomb. The park, that noisy and narrow tract of greenery, had a subterranean smell that seeped from the grates above the underground tracks, mingling with the industrial tang that drifted off the Hudson. I was impressed with the novelty of asphalt pathways strewn with cigarette butts, of bench slats carved by the initialed lovesick, of trash receptacles with improbably dented circumferences. I marveled at the temerity of the squirrels as they ventured up to an outstretched hand that offered bread crusts or peanuts.

I quickly learned one lesson any city child already knew: squirrels were not for petting. During an early visit to the park, I singled out a twitching veteran of other feedings, luring it closer and closer until I could reach down and touch the fur on its back, but the wary rodent kept dodging my hand. Annoyed by the ingratitude, I grabbed for its tail. With a snap, the squirrel scampered free, and in my fingers were the hindmost three inches of its tail. I was thoroughly enlightened by the experience, sorry for the abbreviated animal, but glad not to have been a candidate for rabies immunization.

On the plaza in front of Grant's Tomb, my brother and sister and I roller-skated. My rusty hand-me-downs were clamped fore and aft to my "corrective" brogues with the turn of a key, but the skates kept coming off. Try as I might, I couldn't twist the odd-shaped key forcefully enough for the clamps to really grip, and the leather ankle strap wasn't much help either. The ball bearings in the steel rollers were lacking in lubrication. Moreover, the unevenness of the pavement on the plaza put a damper on anything that resembled an extended glide. The best I could do was a sort of glide-walk, a foxtrot of squealing footfalls that quickly tired my calf muscles.

As I skated, I tried to appreciate the exterior of the monument built to warehouse in perpetuity the recumbent general-president and his wife. To my inexperienced eye, it was the ugliest building I had ever seen. From all angles, it looked neither impressive nor commemorative, but impassive. Its gray stone and stepped, grapefruit-half dome signified inertia—the very thing I was trying to overcome as I struggled across the cracks and against the various frictions. At the time, the tomb was open to the public nearly every day of the year, so, skateless, I would wander inside and wonder at the grim and vaulting waste of space.

Why in heaven's name had they built such a thing? Was this the way Ulysses and Julia chose to ride out eternity, encrypted side by side in oversized red granite sarcophagi? The effect was like two giant shoeboxes in a trash barrel. The Civil War could have been a mound of ashes. The presidency could have been an old tin can. I still can't quite figure out what was being preserved – the bodies or the building materials. Looking back now, as an adult with a more complete knowledge of the details – the dying Grant's terminal bouts with insolvency and throat cancer, and his last great battle, that of penning his autobiography – I reaffirm what I felt when I was ten years old: Grant's Tomb is a failure of a monument, and a monumental failure.

Summer terminated with a search for another apartment, and greater than normal anxiety on my part about returning to school. My father found us a place to live not many blocks away, just off Amsterdam Avenue on 121st Street – at the invisible boundary where Spanish Harlem began and the good gray influence of Columbia University ended. This was a low-rent, racially mixed neighborhood – a world apart from the genteel purlieu of Morningside Heights – and for the first time in my life, my pale skin caused me to be a member of a minority. My native tongue being incomprehensible to most passersby as well, I felt an immediate exclusion from a sense of community. People were assembled everywhere – on the sidewalk, in doorways, on fire escapes – but not our family. With a siege mentality, we navigated between the natives. Vendors unabashedly plied their trade from door to door. There were drunks and there were beggars. Trash collected in the gutters, broken furniture decorated the curbsides, and the curious art of graffiti boomed from the walls.

Our new apartment on the sixth floor of a turn-of-the-century tenement was an elongated "railroad" layout with three bedrooms along an airshaft and a living room that fronted the street. Every window was opaque with grime. A dumbwaiter for the removal of garbage rattled by once a week. Huge, peeling radiators eked out haphazard heat. Floors were splintery, walls hadn't been painted in years. The gas range in the kitchen looked like an early industrial prototype, claw-footed like the bathtub, and the hiss that preceded a burner ring's encirclement of flame scared the daylights out of me. At night, I dreamed of falling asleep and never waking up.

The building's elevator was a paragon of languor. Imprisonment from ground to sixth floor—a good three- or four-minute ride—sometimes verged on terror, especially if the prisoner was alone. The automatic door had a delayed action, so that even after the elevator arrived at its destination, there were prolonged moments of incarceration, moments that made the prisoner lunge for the alarm button. The panicky echo of the bell in the elevator shaft was a reminder not to rely on mechanical contrivances. It was always easier and faster to take the stairs.

My brother and I were enrolled at P.S. 125, an elementary school several blocks crosstown, and it is no exaggeration to say that we were *chased* to and from school every day. (My sister, at P.S. 43, a junior high school farther uptown, had an easier time on the sidewalks of Amsterdam Avenue.) As we hurried through the bleak corner of Morningside Park, my brother and I were prime targets for shakedowns—jeered at, roughed up, and forcibly parted from our lunch money. Briefcase-toting and timorous, we became street-wise only after repeated victimizations. Noting that our first reaction, to trot home and complain tearfully to Mommy, did little to alleviate the situation, we began to sprint through the danger zone. It was a matter of fight or flight. We were no match for the roving gangs of dropouts, but we could run just as fast or faster. I remember my panting, breathless arrivals at school and at home, and interestingly enough, I never felt oppressed; quite the opposite, I rather relished the exercise. I was experiencing the exhilaration of a blockade runner. My plump briefcase of books and schoolwork, my meager pocketful of pennies, my pride—all was delivered intact. I could outrun the bastards.

P.S. 125, formerly Lincoln School, had an enrollment that was a true plebeian hodgepodge. Originally a private institution (and one of academic distinction before it folded), the school had been built to a standard of luxury: it had elevators, a swimming pool, a well-appointed auditorium, even a caged playground on its roof. For several generations, children of upper-class New Yorkers had been educated at Lincoln School, but in the years following World War II, as the neighborhood underwent ethnic change, the white professionals moved out and the school was sold to the city. By the time I was there, the name of Lincoln had been dropped and the old associations were long forgotten. If my mother's reminiscences hadn't brought it to my attention, I don't think I—or any other kid at P.S. 125—would have known or cared about the school's past glory.

I was assigned to a sixth-grade classroom under the tutelage of Mr. Alling, a flat-topped, shiny-suited parvenu who possessed a rectifying sense of purpose. It became clear that I was one of thirty kids sitting in Mr. Alling's inaugural class, although he never told us so. He overflowed with untried ideas; the classroom would be his clinic, and to this end he was constantly adjusting things in pursuit of an imagined harmony — changing our seating, rephrasing questions in mid-sentence, altering an assignment as he wrote it on the blackboard, fooling with the windows and the window shades, taking off and putting on his rayon jacket. He just couldn't sit still.

I think he envisioned the racial rainbow that stared back at him as a teacher's ultimate challenge, and in his excitement he couldn't see the forest for the trees. His ongoing concern was to get us to interact with each other — something we were all doing quite handily, but he never perceived it as such. For all his demonstrative ability, Mr. Alling lacked sensitivity. He didn't know how to communicate on a sixth grader's level. Emotionally, he managed to stiff-arm his charges, and as the school year got underway, my classmates and I responded by generally clamming up. His tinkering, already dispassionate and pointless, became downright heartless. He bullied us at random for answers. He rammed through lessons as though we didn't exist. As the months wore on, Mr. Alling never really bothered to get to know any of us. In order to maintain an aloof pluralism, he chose no teacher's pets, singled out no raised hands (when the braver among us dared to raise our hands). At bottom, I think he was afraid of us. We were certainly afraid of him.

In one of Mr. Alling's restless pedagogical experiments, he rearranged the desks two by two in the classroom so that everyone was paired off in a mix of race and gender. His announced plan was to change the seating arrangement weekly until every possible combination had been effected. My first assigned desk-mate was an African-American girl named Veronica, a thoroughly quiet individual to whom I had paid no previous attention. I was more than a little upset; I had wanted to sit beside Rosa, who was Puerto Rican. From the first day of class, I had been infatuated with Rosa because she wore a full crinoline under her skirt. Barring her, I would have been happy to sit beside Masako, who was Japanese, or Edwina, who was Jewish, both of whom had become cafeteria companions. Another possibility would have been Kerry or Sherry, the freckle-faced twins from Australia (daughters of a diplomat), whose strawberry-blond curls and cheery mannerisms would have been perfect antidotes to the painful classroom proceedings.

As it turned out, Mr. Alling forgot his plan to keep altering the desk arrangement, so for the remainder of the year, I was stuck with Veronica. I did the only thing I could do under the circumstances: I fell in love with her. Her almond eyes, her sensuously flared nostrils, her full lips that curved into a shy smile won over my heart. It didn't take me long to realize that she was the sweetest, funniest person I had ever known. Seated side by side, Veronica and I grew united in loving-kindness, a sharing as well as a meeting of minds. We passed notes all day long. We held hands under our desktops. And it grieved both of us to recognize the fact that we would never be together in subsequent school years, when she would go on to junior high at P.S. 43 and I would return to Rhode Island.

But Mr. Alling committed a less forgivable act of forgetfulness the day he caught me sneaking a ride on an elevator. The elevators were for teachers only (though I'd bet that the privileged kids of yesteryear rode them), and for some reason, Mr. Alling took great offense at my infraction. My riding *his* elevator must have been a personal affront. To see him get so steamed up was scary.

My punishment occurred at the start of lunch period; I was to ascend and descend the six flights of stairs continuously, until he told me to stop. He specifically warned me that *under no circumstance* was I to leave the stairwell until he said to. The man's anger was real.

Well, Mr. Alling went to lunch and promptly forgot about me. With a hanging head, I ascended and descended for twenty minutes, then half an hour, then forty-five minutes. My solitary footfall must have sounded like something out of an Alfred Hitchcock movie. My heart was pounding, I was hungry, and my legs were giving out. After an hour, I heard the class bell: momentarily, there were other kids in the stairwell, and then they were gone. On the verge of tears, I was still climbing up and down. I knew something had gone wrong, and yet I carried out my teacher's orders, blinded by an injured sense of honesty. Although the punishment was already far disproportionate to the crime, I wanted him to know that I was a faithful follower of orders. Wearily, I put one foot ahead of the other. At length, I was barely able to move.

And then Mr. Alling's head appeared at the top of a flight of stairs. "PETER SVENSON! WHY ARE YOU STILL DOING THIS?" he screamed, and the incredulity in his voice crashed against the ceramic brick walls and around the iron treads and handrails. I was crying now.

"You told me not t-to stop until you said to," I stammered.

Mr. Alling's face turned beet red. In my teary fatigue, I was clairvoyant—I could read his mind. He was weighing the penalties for pupil abuse. He knew his nascent teaching career was in jeopardy. He knew his job was on the line if I blabbed. He flew down the stairs to meet me, mumbling a curt apology, and hustled me over to the cafeteria where I was given the dregs of two big aluminum pots just before they were washed. Then he sent me to the nurse's office with a written excuse.

That evening, I told my parents about my ordeal. By then, I was fully recovered, but my account was extremely upsetting to my father. The following morning, he went to P.S. 125 and had a private conference with Mr. Alling. The upshot of their meeting was that for the remainder of the school term I was treated with kid gloves. Never again did I become the object of Mr. Alling's ridicule or wrath. This was the last thing I wanted. It was an unnecessary immunity and a disturbing one. I'm not sure anyone else in the class caught on; to his credit, my ex-tormenter could be subtle when he tried. Still, given his normal behavior, I felt as though I had been singled out for special treatment—a treatment I had not asked for, and neither had my father. But now Mr. Alling was truly afraid of me, afraid of losing his paycheck. For all the wrong reasons, I became the teacher's pet.

NINE

SEVERAL THOUSAND BALES OF HAY are put in the barn annually, and it is my job to sell each one. My goal is an empty barn before cold weather sets in, so that I can take a few months' break before the start of the next growing season. All spring and summer, I have been making hay—mowing, raking, baling, and transporting wagon loads to the barn. More often than not, it has been a good crop year. I have breathed hay's halcyon aroma as my helpers and I stacked bale after bale as high and higher than the roof eaves. I have sneezed and I have sweated, and, finally, I have experienced the satisfaction of seeing the hay mows full. Following this, I have ventilated the barn on sunny days—rolling open the big doors in the morning, closing them in the evening. Lastly, I have planted my Hay For Sale sign beside the highway, and placed a twelve-word ad in the "Feed-Seed-Fert." column of the classifieds. I am ready to make a little money.

My hay customers hail from all walks of life. They come in cattle trucks, pickups, horse vans, eighteen-wheelers, tractor-drawn farm wagons, and any other conveyance that will hold hay bales in quantity. Their common goal is the winter feeding of animals. Some customers are close neighbors, but most live elsewhere in the county, and a few travel from communities fifty miles away and farther. Normally I am telephoned in advance, although I welcome spur-of-the-moment customers, too. Word gets out that I have square bales for sale—something of a rarity these days when most of the local hay is round baled. Modern twelve-hundred-pound rolls are the efficiency experts' answer to the old-fashioned, forty-pound rectilinear bales by a factor of thirty to one. I fill the market need of the small-scale hay customer, who's feeding only a few animals and doesn't have the equipment to handle the big round bales.

Because of the steady pilgrimage to my barn, beginning in late summer and continuing into fall, my sales technique has undergone noticeable improvement. Five years ago, when I began selling hay, my marketing skills were minimal; I stood in the barn and tried to look friendly. I was quiet, trusting, uncharismatic. That selling was distasteful to me must have been written all over my face. I wasn't used to transacting with strangers.

Having retired to the country on three previous occasions to live the contemplative life and eke a livelihood from my creativity, I had never placed myself so directly in the middle of the cash flow. As a painter, I was relying upon those profit-halving go-betweens, the commercial galleries, to keep me in funds. My job was to paint the canvases and deliver them to the service entrances. The fifty-percent commission a gallery lopped off the price of a painting was supposed to spare me the headache of dickering. The pretentiousness of this arrangement would have worked fine—and justified itself—if my paintings had been selling well. As it is, my paintings have always sold poorly. Months, even years go by when not a single canvas is bought. To pay for my basic necessities, I've had to resort to other schemes; one in particular I can't look back on without a smirk of irony, for in order to make headway as an artist, I've literally had to sell my heritage.

Soon after graduating from college I began hawking antiques and other family heirlooms that had been handed down to me with the understanding that I would cherish them in perpetuity. My parents regularly de-accessioned the contents of their seemingly bottomless closets and endless shelves—but there was a catch: my sister and brother and I were supposed to hold onto these hand-me-downs and pass them on to our own children and grandchildren. Fortunately, it was a catch I could circumvent without guilt; I felt no attachment whatsoever to these revered possessions.

Albatrosses don't wear well around my neck. Early on, I had decided that the major collectibles in my life would come from my own hand. My unsold paintings leaning against the wall and piled under the bed were what I really wanted to preserve. I was running out of room and patience. My plan was to jettison the heavy boxes jammed with the knickknacks of yesteryear, all lovingly padded with crushed newspaper, and labeled and sealed f.o.b. eternity. So I carried around the old clocks, the crystal bowls, the Limoges dinner set, the turn-of-the-century figurines to antique dealers, and eked a modest supplement from time to time to get me over the humps.

But even then I entered in the spirit of the bazaar not because I wanted to, but because I had to. I remember how sleazy it felt to walk into a musty shop on the seedier side of town with an heirloom or two tucked under my arm. That the proprietor would consider relieving me of these treasures was my most fervent desire. I tried to impersonate a scion of failed wealth, so as not to give the impression that my goods were "hot." More often than not, the dealer would orchestrate a crescendo of put-downs, criticizing the commonness of my wares, pointing out their flaws, and concluding with an unenthusiastic offer that seemed to vary between a third and a quarter of what I thought the things were worth. Meekly, I'd accept the terms. Later (or the next time I needed to flog an item), I'd return to the shop only to find that my unspoken estimate was indeed the price on the sales sticker. The fine line between markup and highway robbery was crossed many times, but I never made it my business to complain.

When remaining solvent was at its most burdensome, I held jobs in the retail sector. I functioned ably enough, but my heart wasn't in it. The longest I ever stayed in sales was at a furniture store in Charlottes-ville, a hip purveyor of butcherblock and polystyrene, where I stood around and reinforced customers' poor taste with murmurings of ap-proval. To repay a construction loan, I worked there for about a year. Right from the start, it seemed an appalling waste of time and talent to be present on the sales floor from ten to six, bearing witness to the inde-cision of others, but like any other endeavor, it began to grow on me. Analyzed in retrospect, my dissatisfaction wasn't so much with the job as it was with the remuneration. I wasn't selling on commission; at my piddling hourly wage, it didn't matter if I conned customer A or cus-tomer Z into springing for the rose-patterned hide-a-bed. I could have sold dozens more davenports if the incentive had been right.

That's one thing to be said for the selling of hay bales—I'm paid on commission. Deducting the expenses of tractor fuel, lubricants, baling twine, student help, and my own long hours in the field, each bale represents cash in the pocket. And although my forty-acre hay operation hardly qualifies as a booming business, its slender margin of income keeps the wolves from our door. Best of all, I am my own boss. I've learned to pat myself on the back for a job well done.

In hay selling season, I try to arrange the barn like a showroom of sorts. I keep it orderly and well swept, with at least a portion of its main floor empty so customers can back right in for loading. The two tractors, the baler, and the mower-conditioner are parked cheek by jowl in the remaining space (the haywagon is in a stall below and the rake is next door in a machine shed). The stepped walls of hay that rise in the mows to the left and right are redolent with summer past. On a wooden peg I display two ribbons—a white one for third premium, a blue one for first premium—won in hay competitions at the county fair. My not-so-subliminal message is quality as well as quantity.

Hay customers are most readily categorized as farmers and non-farmers. Nonfarming customers tend to be curious about how the hay gets from field to bale. They want to know the exact percentage of clover, of orchardgrass, of fescue, of weeds—as though a list of ingredients were something their animals might want to consider as they ruminate, like the nutritional information on a cereal box. I try to assuage their curiosity with figures: 15 percent, 45 percent, 35 percent, 5 percent. My educated guesses and their assenting nods are steps in the courting dance that precedes our transaction. Then, too, they want to know how "good" the hay is (they have no skills for assessing this on their own), so I show them the ribbons and tell them quite frankly that, were I a horse, I would eat it myself.

The farmers, on the other hand, are too savvy to succumb to such direct civility. They know what they're looking for, and they go about finding it in a circumspect way. As I walk with them into the barn, likely as not they're relating some complaint about the weather. The hay is eyed with sidelong glances while the commentary shifts to my rolling stock, or to the hay elevator propped against the wall ("Haven't seen one of those things in years!"). After additional preliminaries elapse, a closer inspection of the bales is accompanied by a barely disguised grunt of disapproval over their size and weight, then once again, attention is shunted to another topic. At this point, I know I haven't long to wait. They'll take a pickup load or a trailer load—sometimes they'll commit themselves to an entire mowful —or they'll turn me down cold.

Because I have set my price in advance (between a dollar and two dollars a bale), the niceties of barter are dispensed with. The price of hay depends on the size of the cutting and its quality. I stand ready with a whittled pencil and a scrap of something to write on. All office appurtenances are banned from the barn. There are no calculators, no ballpoint pens, no pads of paper, no paperclips. I do my math in longhand. The tractor hood or the housing of the mower-conditioner is my desk. For the people who pay cash, I don't even make change. I like to keep things simple, I strive to project an earthy directness that suits the scope and scale of hay farming. That way, customers don't feel threatened by my Yankee accent or grammatical precision. Later, back at the house, I'll do my record-keeping.

74

Ideally, the loading of hay is a joint effort. I'm in the mow, tossing down the bales—and calling out the count loud and clear—while the buyer stacks them on his or her backed-in vehicle. On many occasions, though, I wind up doing most, if not all the labor by myself, which I don't mind in the least. As an experienced bale handler, I heft bales by the hundreds and suffer no ill effects; in fact, I take a proprietary pleasure in handling the bales one last time before they are carted away. Each forty-pound bundle of dried leaf and bloom encinched by two bands of twine becomes an object of fleeting contemplation. The important thing is to take my time and not lose count.

People have a tendency to make light of the fact that a ton of hay weighs as much as a ton of bricks. A tall load of bales on a vehicle, no matter how overlapped its bond, is at the mercy of centrifugal force from the first forgetfully accelerated bend. Picking up fallen bales on the road-way is both an embarrassment and a hazard. Loads will shift, too, because of bumps and jolts. Drooping lopsidedly, an off-centered load of hay can contribute to the loss of control—and possible overturning—of a wagon or a truck. The experienced customer sees to it that the bales are stacked tightly, short of overloading, and that the resultant mass is properly lashed down. The experienced customer brings his or her own rope. For the uninitiated, I always keep a supply of twine strands handy (from broken bales), which can be spliced together for temporary tie-downs.

The selling of hay affords me plenty of opportunity to cluck my tongue over the nearsightedness of human nature. Farmers aside, most people with animals don't stockpile hay for the duration of the feeding season. This may be attributable to lack of storage space as well as lack of funds. One long-standing customer of mine feeds his donkeys the very last bale before he comes over for more. Another fellow, a riding stable proprietor, buys a pickup load when he claims to be desperate, but he never pays for it until a day or two later, which makes me suspect he is re-selling the hay to someone else. And with the first flurries of winter, my phone sometimes rings off the hook, for the prospect of snow-covered pastures suddenly reminds animal owners that their feed supply is running low. Unfortunately for them, my barn is usually empty by then.

My customers, for the most part, are wholesome individuals whose commitment to buy hay (and pay cash on the barrel) is sincere. In every season, though, a crook or two comes calling. Now, after five years in the business, I can usually unmask the deceivers—the ones who come over without any money, the ones who weasel out of a promised purchase, the ones who telephone ahead, asking me to hold a big order, then never show up. Far from discouraging me, the occasional bad experience enhances my resiliency as an entrepreneur. The agricultural marketplace is rough and tumble; courage and a gut feeling for competition are necessary for survival. Somewhere along the line I have dropped my reserved, reticent attitude toward the people who beat a path to my barn. The long hours in the field have toughened me up. I've learned to make damn good hay. I believe in my product as I believe in myself. I perfect my sales pitch even as I perfect my love for my fellow human beings.

But in the cautionary recesses of my mind, I'll always preserve one incident that occurred during my first full summer in the tractor seat, when I had a bumper crop of hay and an equally large measure of inexperience.

A prosperous-looking fellow in a new pickup truck drove up to the barn one day and proceeded to tell me his life story. He was recently re-married, he said, and he and his bride had just purchased a working fifty-acre cattle farm. They didn't know a thing about farming. He was a salesperson at a prominent car dealership in Harrisonburg. She taught kindergarten or something. Their pastures were overgrazed and the cattle were starving. Would my hay be alright for them? How many bales should he feed? Would I sell him a trial pickup load, and if the cows liked it, could he come by for a couple of loads a month *on a permanent basis?*

I was flattered with questions. A permanent customer is a joy forever. I answered that I'd be happy to sell him all the hay he needed, accommodating his queries with my old furniture store affability, salesperson to salesperson, for here was a kindred spirit. We gabbed about farming and painting as we loaded the hay. He paid cash to the penny, promising to return during the following week. Dazed by his attention and interest, I watched him drive away, his showroom-shiny truck overburdened with the abundance of my showroom of hay.

A week went by, then two. There was no sign of him. At the start of the third week, I began to worry about when he would reappear. Maybe his cows had strange taste buds, maybe he found a better deal elsewhere. Then one afternoon he came bouncing down the lane, his tanned face grinning appreciatively. Man, that was some mighty fine hay I sold him, he said. His cows had gone nuts over the stuff; in fact, he couldn't keep them away from the truck as he unloaded – they chomped craters in the bales, they loved it so much. Could he get five or six more loads right away?

"Why, sure," I said. "Take as many loads as you want."

But it turned out he didn't have his checkbook. He asked if he could write the check when he came for the final load. He joked that one big check was just as good as a lot of little checks. Reluctantly, I agreed.

And so he drove out with another load, and another, and another, and still another, and he promised to be back in the morning for two more loads, and he *wouldn't forget* his checkbook.

A more astute person than I would have spotted the set-up. I was being reeled in hook, line, and sinker. I fully expected him to return, and of course, he didn't. He never came back. I called his home and office (the consummate salesperson, he had provided me with both phone numbers), but at each place he had "just stepped out." I left my name and number. He never returned the calls. I didn't want it to look like I was pestering him, so I waited—a day, a week, two weeks.

The grace period of my patience having run out, I decided to dial him again. Miraculously, I got through. Instant bonhomie boomed across the wire. *Where had I been*, he asked? He had tried to reach me at least ten times. He needed more hay. He'd be over that evening, and he'd write a check to cover the full amount he owed.

Again, he failed to reappear. I sent him carefully typewritten bills with "Past Due" underlined in red. I telephoned now and then, and when I succeeded in getting past the receptionist and/or message machine, I got the recurrent litany: yes, he was coming over, he'd say, but I had to understand that he was *an extremely busy man*. When I contacted him a couple of weeks later, he introduced a new theme. He'd send the check in the mail. He had just written it; in fact, it was sitting on his desk. By this time, there was no mention of coming back for more hay.

Well, more than a month went by in this vein. A second month passed. The three hundred and some dollars he owed wafted in a netherworld between my mailbox-anticipation and his grifter's conscience. It was not the fault of the Postal Service. He never sent the check. He had no intention of ever sending a check. The rip-off was a fait accompli. I felt duped, betrayed. He had strung me along as far as he deemed necessary. He could have given any excuse, and I would have believed him. He could have offered to pay in installments, and I would have bent over backward to accommodate his terms. But four large pickup loads of hay just going poof!—it was too big an investment of time and hard work to write off. He probably thought I'd forgive and forget. Well, I just couldn't.

The catalyst for my resolution of this distasteful situation was my mother-in-law, who was visiting Becky and me one weekend in late fall. A plain-speaking, farm-bred woman from the tobacco country of North Carolina, she listened to my account of the hay-thieving and volunteered an easy solution: I should go to the car dealership and demand my money. If the salesperson balked, I should raise a stink with his boss. To heck with letters and phone calls!

It was a solution I had previously dismissed as being too reprehensible, for by this time the last thing I wanted was another glimpse of the salesperson's two-timing mug. Besides, I was not a confrontational kind of guy. But the more I thought about it, I understood my mother-in-law's wisdom. My showing up at the man's workplace would force him to save face. It was a cheap shot. I had to take it.

So I got up my nerve and drove to the car dealership, parking my dilapidated pickup squarely in the middle of the glossy ranks. I marched through the glass doors, ignoring the simpering may-I-help-you's, and headed straight toward the cubicle with my debtor's name on the door. He was there all right, sitting behind his desk in his lair of third-rate prints and training awards, and his jaw dropped an ill-concealed fraction as he looked up.

"Mr. Svenson, how nice to see you. As a matter of fact, I just tried calling you about an hour ago . . ."

There were no pleasantries on my part. "I've come to collect the money you owe me, which is . . ." and I recited the exact amount.

By my overly loud enunciation, he knew that I meant business. He knew I would have screamed if he so much as uttered a waffling word.

"Why of course, Mr. Svenson. I'll do it right now." And as I glared at him, he bent over his desktop, on which his smiling bride and his children from his previous marriage conspired good-naturedly, and extracted his big folio checkbook from a drawer. His performance was as fluid and flawless as the script from his felt-tipped pen. But handing the check to me, and glinting with anger at losing the game he had fully intended to win, he couldn't resist a final riposte, and that was to tell me how his cows hadn't really liked my hay all that much.

I turned my back on him in a righteous huff. Waves of relief were threatening to twist my frown into a grin. I escaped the car lot and headed straight for the bank. And after that, it got easier—the selling, I mean. This is my secret: I never let another person out-sell me on my own turf.

TEN

In the spring of 1955, when my father's sabbatical year in New York City ended, we vacated our apartment on 121st Street and moved back to West Kingston. The year away from Rhode Island made it seem paradisiacal to me. Descending from the train at Kingston station was like stepping back into a dimension I had left only physically; spiritually, I seemed to have never gone away. The old station's Victorian overhang, its granite-post-and-iron-pipe turnaround beside the overpass of Route 138, were referents I had clung to when I was gone, as if the thought of them would ensure safe passage home, which I guess it did.

The station taxi, a wood-paneled Willys, conveyed us along Railroad Avenue and Waites Corner Road, a route so familiar to my pedaling feet that I forgot for a moment that I hadn't ridden a bicycle for a year. Everything was the same—Jimmy Harvey's house, the West Kingston School, Kathy Kelly's house, the Grillos'. Kenyon's ice cream parlor, purveyor of my favorite treat—a ten-cent pistachio cone—had expanded its parking lot, but we didn't have time to stop. Savoring the green confection in my mind, I sloughed off the year in Manhattan. When the taxi turned into our sandy lane, it was as if the red carpet had been rolled out; I wanted to reach out the window and touch the profusion of nature, the welcoming committee of elderberry, wild cherry, and sumac that brushed the sides of the car and ingratiated itself in the right of way. Even the brambles and poison ivy beckoned a forked greeting.

Home was as we had left it, more or less, the difference being the furniture the tenants (a faculty family) had temporarily left behind. This was a collection of 1950s modern, the antithesis of my parents' boring old accoutrements which were stored in the basement. In the living room now stood a kidney-shaped, rod-legged coffee table—as stark a piece of furniture as I had ever seen. There was also a blond wood phonograph cabinet, the Victrola equivalent of Marilyn Monroe, crammed with new LP's, mostly jazz. A brick and plank bookshelf of bric-a-brac and best sellers stood against the wall where the old dining-room sideboard had been. Upstairs in my parents' bedroom was an actual television set (my parents wouldn't purchase one for another three years) and canvas-and-steel sling chairs, indo red and kelly green, that were amazingly comfortable to sit in. As I embraced the old habitat, I embraced these futuristic furnishings I'd seen only in window displays and magazine advertisements, but I felt a certain amount of confusion, too. The year in New York had put me off balance; I felt "out of it," as the expression went. The microcosm of West Kingston had preserved itself while I was away, but now that I was back, I was confronted with its changes, and the biggest change of all was in me. I could no longer look at 1920s-era neo-Victorian furniture and be unmindful of its ugliness.

Our Kaiser sedan, nosed into the garage for the duration (after delivering us to New York City, my father had driven it back alone), was restored to life with jumper cables by Rocky Taylor, the local Cities Service mechanic. Belching and misfiring, it was dispatched to the new supermarket in Wakefield to replenish the kitchen cupboard. Back in New York, I had bragged to my classmates that my parents owned a car, and no one had believed me. (City kids couldn't fathom a backyard of twenty-seven acres, either.) Eagerly, my brother and sister and I separated the leaning tangle of bicycles at the back of the garage and pumped up the almost-flat tires. Only by riding around in individual pilgrimages of reacquaintance could we overcome the strangeness of the missing year, and take up where we had left off.

I looked forward to seventh grade and the opportunity to be reunited with my classmates from Kingston Grammar School, but Mrs. Hilliard's seventh-grade classroom above the kindergarten wing was no longer there. During the time we were away, the county school system had been restructured to coincide with the completion of the South Kingstown School. County-wide, all children in grades seven through twelve were being bused to the new facility. I wasn't distressed in the least; having weathered so many changes so recently, I was perfectly capable of withstanding one more. With aplomb, my sister and I rode the schoolbus six miles to Wakefield where the pristine school sat on a couple of acres of freshly unrolled turf. Being a lowly seventh grader in a busload of "upper classmen" didn't faze me, either. There I sat—shorter, younger, and my voice hadn't dropped—but I considered myself to be a person of no small experience. The jolting, jarring progress of the bus only ratified my sense of importance: *the bus had stopped for me*. Every mile of ear-splitting teenage cacophony bolstered my self-confidence.

Seventh grade got off to a satisfactory start. I quickly forgot I was the youngest member of the class. I adapted well to the novel system of homerooms and class periods. The sprawling building incorporated an up-to-date functionality—green blackboards and aluminum chalk rails, "ice-tray" fluorescent fixtures and vinyl-tiled floors, louvered windows with heating units recessed in the wall beneath them, molded plastic desks and chairs. I could see that all these things were designed to stream-line the learning process. I couldn't help but be a good student. I made straight A's. I made lots of new friends. I continued with clarinet (to pre-serve the memory of Adah, who had moved away), but I also took up the B-flat horn. I undertook an ambitious science fair project, one that involved the identification of every kind of tree on our property in West Kingston. I marched in the school band, I went to dances, took piano lessons, attended football games, and I fell in love two, maybe three times.

Thinking back to this happy and hectic school year, I realize it was my last hurrah of childhood, a prelude to adolescence. It was a year of renewal and full-circle fulfillment, but it was also a year of discontinuity, for it began at the railroad station and ended at Rocky Taylor's service station as he filled the Kaiser's gas tank for a one-way trip to New Jersey. Our family was moving away again, this time for good.

The year had been a necessary delay to allow my father to collect his teaching salary at URI while finishing his doctoral thesis at NYU. He was fed up with Rhode Island, and my mother was too. The sabbatical in New York had reawakened their cherished notion that he deserved a better job. Neither of my parents had really embraced the idea of sink-ing roots in New England's glacial till. Rhode Island was temporary. It had stayed temporary for eight years. My siblings and I were well aware of the ongoing parental uneasiness with our surroundings—our drafty domicile on untameable acreage near a second-rate university, as they termed it. Although they had adapted as best they could, they were ur-ban creatures at heart. They pined for the environs of New York City— its Culture with a capital C, its bustle.

The green light to get out of Rhode Island came with the long-awaited doctorate. My father was offered, and he accepted, an assistant profes-sorship at New York University's graduate school of business adminis-tration. Our one-way ticket out of the "backwater" had finally arrived.

To their credit, my mother and father understood the advantages of country living with respect to bringing up children. It would have been hard for them not to have noticed the positive effects on my brother and sister and me; we were contented, well-adjusted kids. Clearly, we were thriving in Rhode Island. Nor had my parents forgotten the traumas of the New York City school system, and the hassle and expense of living in Manhattan. A happy medium was decided upon. We would find a place to live in a bedroom community in New Jersey, right across the Hudson River, a fast rail or bus commute away.

Having the means (his pending professorship) to secure a mortgage, my father bought a house in Montclair—hometown of his mentors Gilbreth and Drucker—a slender, Tennessee-shaped wedge of suburb surrounded by others of its kind, spread against the first of a series of hogbacks that paralleled the Hudson River, thirteen miles away. It was a town of wealth and trees, with streets rising to its ridge that were lined with great, sprawling estates, products of a less egalitarian era when businessmen hired servants and maintained tennis courts. Streets were named for stratospheric effect—Afterglow Way, Upper Mountain Avenue, Crestmont Road. The boom years of the 1920s had engendered the English Tudor mansions and rambling castles of brick that now hid behind rhododendrons, distanced by wrought-iron fences, seemingly occupied by nobody but elderly lingerers. Popular personalities of the celluloid era had lived in Montclair—cult evangelists, displaced royalty, insurance magnates.

But Montclair was a town that also included in its nether reaches (along Bloomfield Avenue in the direction of New York City and adjacent, more plebeian townships) a substantial black community—the foundation, as it were, for the upper crust. The servant- and working-class lived in clapboard firetraps on streets that did not bear poetic names. Here was Maple Avenue, Mission Street, the parallel Grant and Sherman Streets. Our new residence was a three-story stucco structure in the buffer zone between the enclaves of wealth and poverty, at the corner of Union Street and Prospect Terrace in a densely built neighborhood that had seen better days. It was a part of town that was gradually being rebuilt with apartment houses because it was a short walk from the town center and Lackawanna Station, where olive-drab, straw-seated trains shuttled regularly to Newark and Hoboken.

We moved in during the heat of summer. My brother and I were assigned the two bedrooms on the stifling third floor, a former servants' quarters. There under the eaves, we shared the servants' bathroom, a glorified closet illuminated by an electrified gas lamp. Its window was low to the floor right beside the toilet, and it didn't occur to my brother or me to pull the shade until our next door neighbor tactfully complained.

The second floor had two large bedrooms—one for my sister, the other for my parents—two bathrooms, a library with a study off one end (that soon acquired the persistent haze of my father's cigarette smoke), and numerous still-functioning mother-of-pearl wall buttons to summon the servants of yesteryear. An oak-bannistered stairway descended to the entrance foyer via a raised landing where the telephone and the finer antiques from my mother's side of the family were displayed. The first floor salons were paneled in dark oak (cherry in the dining room) with false beamwork on their ceilings. A massive picture molding and china rail made every wall amenable to additional objects of decoration. Behind swinging doors between the dining room and kitchen was a butler's pantry—a nook with ceiling-high, glass-fronted cabinets and an oddly shaped sink in its green linoleum countertop. Off the dining room and living room was a sun porch, in which screened or glass-paned inserts could be installed as the season demanded.

Dating from around 1910, the house was reputed to have been built for a retired mayor of Montclair, a widower who had spurned the family mansion farther up the hill. Half a century later, these bachelor quarters seemed absolutely palatial. Their somber interior, shaded by long-established yews and hemlocks, was soundproofed almost to the point of being spooky. The house was so solid, so compartmentalized that when you closed a door behind you, you were entirely alone. A petit bourgeois luxury exuded from every detail—the newel posts, the travertine fireplaces, the sliding double doors, the system of servants' bells and speaking tube between kitchen and second floor, the gaslights and leaded panes. There were forty-three windows in the house, and each one was numbered with a little engraved marker on the sill.

From the outside, the house was faintly Moorish in appearance, with overweening soffits and archwork above the entranceways and prominent windows, and its corners did not go perpendicularly to the ground, but flared slightly at foundation level. Long after we moved in, I'd find myself studying the house from various angles in its tiny yard and being struck by its exoticism, and I'd ask myself the obvious rhetorical question: what was a house like this doing in New Jersey?

But the feature of the house I appreciated most was its basement, a dank and whitewashed catacomb that surpassed any basement I had ever seen. The stairway leading to it was a plain, wide descent painted battle-ship gray, and it ended at a landing that turned both left and right, giving access to a maze of partitioned space. Beneath the stairway, a few worn garden tools communed in the shadows. In the largest room, a three-tubbed laundry facility with spider-webbed washboards propped along a soapstone drainboard looked perennially ready for use. Across from it stood a workbench like a slightly raised funeral bier. The furnace room was dominated by an Etruscan-red oil burner of impressive bulk. Its predecessor necessitated the three or four adjacent coal bunkers, rooms unto themselves, where leftover heaps of anthracite had been swept into the corners. A cryptic antechamber off to one side held the house shut-ters, all carefully numbered, in permanent storage. Beside the outdoor bulkhead was a solitary commode in a beaded-board enclosure illumi-nated by a dangling bulb on a pull chain, the perfect refuge for reading in privacy.

Awaiting school, knowing nobody, and desirous of minimizing the oppressively hot New Jersey summer, I spent most of my time in the basement. With my parents' uncomprehending consent, I began tearing down the partitioning between the coal bunkers, my goal being the creation of a rumpus room. Wielding a sledge hammer, I bashed the splintery boards apart, assiduously removing the nails and stacking the lumber for future use (I was envisioning an art-framing business, among other projects). Then I repainted the foundation walls, scoured the con-crete floor, screwed brighter bulbs in the ceiling sockets. My brother was given a ping pong table for his eleventh birthday, which fit nicely into my general scheme. On the cleaned concrete, I set about delineating a shuffleboard court. Pucks and sticks were fashioned from the lumber pile. Lastly, I affixed a basketball hoop to the stair railing. I was preserv-ing the untrammeled productiveness that living on twenty-seven acres had fostered, the only difference being that now I did it underground.

But my involvement in these subterranean improvements, and their subsequent recreational enjoyment, only hastened the first day of school. I began eighth grade at Hillside Junior High, six blocks away, a columned edifice that reflected Montclair's strong tax base and com-mitment to public education. Subduing my newcomer's self-conscious-ness—abetted by pimples and erections and octave-unsure crackings in my voice—I made every effort to forge acquaintances. The town's wealth notwithstanding, many of my classmates were from the lower socioeconomic echelons, kids who lived on the downside of Montclair's bi-polar personality like myself and didn't walk home to half-timbered manses set back from the street.

In fact, Hillside School turned out to be exactly the opposite of what I would have expected it to be. On the outside, with its columns and tan brick pediments, the school looked loftily generic, evoking the narcissism of its generous civic endowment. "O thou Hillside, thy books, thy halls, thy classrooms . . ." began the school song—a corruption of "Londonderry Air"—before it trailed off in verses that promised eternal devotion and unflagging gratitude. But inside, the school was a beehive of diversity. Nobody, including the teachers, agreed on anything. An everyday subject like math or English was as unpredictable as the weather. The place was bubbling, pluralistic; both sides of any discussion were sure to be aired. Occasionally, fights erupted in the halls, or food fights in the cafeteria, but for all its abrasive contradictions, there was an integrity about the school that appealed to me. It mirrored Montclair in a way that looked beyond the town's prestigious name and made-up face. Montclair was both a heaven and a hell, and Hillside provided an education for the teenaged constituents of both realms.

I looked forward to the school day as never before. I found myself able to make friends and enemies with equanimity; enemies turned into friends and vice versa. A curious state of flux was the norm. Opposites held sway. In shop class, I made a toy sailboat and then a full-sized crossbow. In print class, I cycled between Old English and Dom Casual. In art class I concocted the required still lifes and winter sport scenes, then switched to cheesecake, confiscated as it was passed around the room. I learned to weave on a loom. I learned the subjunctive and the pluperfect. In civics debates, I mastered the convincing expulsion of hot air ("Resolved: Who was the Greater President? Washington or Lincoln").

And after school, I became adept at caroming through the fast-paced suburban environment, that pastiche of the commercial and the residential, punctuated by ubiquitous trees—I got to know my way around. Hitting the trail by foot or by bike as soon as the dismissal bell rang, my first stop was the newsstand or the drugstore, where pennies paid for some saccharine reward: bubblegum, popsicle, or candy bar. Then I cruised through the municipal park, just in case a pickup game of baseball or touch football was in progress. Then I toured along the main drag, Bloomfield Avenue, including forays inside the music store and the camera store. The bicycle shop was next on my agenda, followed by a return to the drugstore for a soda and to check on who was hanging out, and with whom. My next stop was the public library, where I worked part-time shelving books. Two hours later, I'd be heading home for supper and homework.

Thirty-six *years* later, I strive hard to preserve that fullness of life in which every minute added to the vocabulary of experience. In the evenings now, though I manage to eschew television, I'm content to prop my feet on the couch and scan the newspaper or flip through a magazine. During those evenings in Montclair, I sequestered myself on the third floor with a filched Do Not Disturb sign on my doorknob. Therein, the fullness continued. Impatiently, I'd execute my homework, eager for more cognitive employment. I was a collector of old radios and radio tubes, a fixer of clocks and phonographs. One half of my desktop was set aside for the building of model planes. I flew, I crashed, I rebuilt. I also dabbled in chemistry. With small amounts of chemical contraband, I manufactured my own gunpowder and rocket propellant, expanding my line of homemade pyrotechnics to include Roman candles and catherine wheels. I also repaired fishing reels. I practiced photography on the side; my darkroom was an unused closet on the second floor, my developing trays were my mother's Pyrex baking dishes. I did sewing projects on an ancient sewing machine I rescued from a neighbor's trash. Only when it came time to turn in, did I read myself to sleep.

My first two years in Montclair passed in this occupational plenitude. The world was my Erector set, my Tinkertoy. If any part of it moved, or lit up, or came apart, or spewed forth something else, I was interested. I was at a loss for spare time. I began to see that our move to New Jersey was, indeed, a step forward; now I had mobility of purpose and the means to do just about anything I wanted to. More and more, I was my own person. School was fine, life was fine. By observing the ground rules—like getting home in time for supper and getting up in the morning—I could structure my day so that it teemed with activity. The more I got to know the other kids in school, the more interesting they became, too. My friendships crossed every artificial divide. There were dancing classes at the Montclair Women's League on Friday nights, sock hops at the Y on Saturday nights, Pilgrim Fellowship meetings at the Congregational church on Sunday nights, and plenty of afternoon sessions at the bowling alley and the movies. I got invited to make-out parties where the orientation of an empty soda bottle on the floor dictated whom you were to kiss, and for how long. I listened (and jitterbugged) as the music of Elvis elbowed its way beyond the tame formulations of Como and Clooney.

As I finished ninth grade, I was excited about the prospect of going to Montclair High School. Everyone was excited! My classmates and I had made the long haul together. We'd be going to one of the finest damn high schools around, home of a helluva football team, et cetera. It was hard for me to believe my steam-rolling good luck. Or was it pluck? At any rate, I was about to embark upon the best of all possible futures, and before long—three more years, to be precise—*I would be free.*

One blustery spring afternoon, I stood in the schoolyard at Hillside and flew a balsa glider, a craft of my own design painted yellow with a sixteen-inch wingspan. It was the best glider I had ever made, an easy-to-throw fast-climber that stayed and stayed, circling predictably until it ran out of altitude. A veteran of many such afternoons, its stick fuselage had been broken and reglued in several places, and nicks and notches marred the leading edges of its wings and elevator.

I had been launching it for more than an hour, and I was almost ready to quit. Flight after flight—five circles, sometimes six—it floated splendidly on the air before brushing the ground and cartwheeling to rest. The ball of modeling clay on its nose (for weight and to soften the landing) was a snub deformity stuck with bits of grass and dirt. Retrieving the plane, I reshaped its nose ball once again, and with a balancing pinch, I gave the fuselage one final upwind heave. But this time, even as I released it, I sensed that the wind velocity and launch trajectory were imbued with a magical equilibrium. The glider shot straight into the sky, and as it began circling, it held its altitude. Alone in the schoolyard, I stood there, the vicarious pilot with his neck craned, but instead of gliding downward, the little airplane rose in a somnolent gyre and drifted beyond the confines of the chain-link fence. Higher and higher it soared, now well above the danger of Montclair's trees. It looked like a high-flying, serene canary or a runaway helium balloon. It became a dot, then a speck, and then it disappeared.

There on the ground, I thought how wonderful it would be to waft on such a wind as I gained experience along my way to adulthood, which did not seem so distant anymore or so difficult to fathom in its meaning and complexity. I had just turned fourteen.

ELEVEN

THROUGH FOUR GROWING SEASONS I make hay on the battleground, barely noticing the slight but accumulating decline in the hay tonnage from year to year as the soil grows acidic and loses fertility. I have left the fields pretty much as I found them (aside from the fence-line alterations) because I know the dire consequences of overenrichment of farmland. The algae-choked pond at the bottom of the hill is prima facie evidence that neighbors upstream are overfertilizing. Six years have passed, and I haven't gotten used to the algal invasion. I still expect to see the water's reflective surface, but in its place – nine days out of ten – I find the shocking-green plane, a free-form billiard table.

The low input farming methods to which I aspire have led to harvests that fall below bumper expectations, crop stands short of the proverbial elephant's eye. I'm satisfied with the results, though. My watchword is stewardship. All along, my idea has been to make money but not make a killing.

And yet it is plain to see that our fields are gradually losing their fecundity. The rightful occupants of the sod – orchard grass, red clover, and fescue – are giving way to weeds, but there are added complications. Because of its vigor, the fescue has been crowding out the orchard grass, putting the proportions of the hay mix out of balance. Fescue makes a good winter pasture, but only marginal summer hay. Broomsedge, that peach-colored indicator of low pH, feathers in the wind in broad sections of the fields now. Johnsongrass, quack grass, and chicory are established, too. To a practiced eye, the fields can be read like a book; this chapter is entitled, "The Decline of the Soil."

It is time to lime and fertilize the fields, for starters. All it takes is a phone call (and money). The lime truck and the fertilizer truck will grind across the acreage, spreading the contents of their hoppers in thirty-foot swaths. Lime dust coats the fields, billowing in chalky clouds from the spinning broadcaster at the rear of the truck. Fertilizer comes in pellets, similarly spread, or in a liquid sprayed from hinged, elongated booms. The procedure is over in minutes, and for the first few weeks, before the greening jumpstart becomes apparent, all I see is a fat withdrawal in the checkbook ledger.

Area farmers who raise cattle, hogs, or poultry fertilize with in-house waste, as it were. (An option not available to me; the only animals I raise at the moment are cats.) Poultry litter, smelling to high heaven, spreads like pelletized fertilizer, but it is not recommended for hayfields because poultry feed contains weed seeds that, having passed through digestive systems, are ripe for sprouting. Animal manure can be spread the old-fashioned way with a tractor-drawn spreader, but more often these days, it is conveyed to holding tanks or pits where it is mixed with water to form a slurry, then applied to the fields by that nemesis of a fragrant morning, the "honey wagon." The trouble is that the volume of in-house waste usually exceeds the in-house fertilizer requirement, especially on animal-intensive farms where loafing lots and poultry barns are the mainstays of the operation. A tendency to overfertilize is not uncommon in the agribusiness-ridden Shenandoah Valley; throwing fertilizer around is cheaper than throwing money around, and it gets results just as fast. But the soil will absorb only so much of it, so the rest of the stuff runs downhill, fanning out in the floating green stranglehold, ultimately altering (according to experts) the ecosystem of faraway Chesapeake Bay.

There comes a point, though, when all the fertilizer in the world won't help to raise a better crop. Two of my four large hayfields are too weed-infested to spend another dollar on the nitrogen-phosphate-potash pellets. What I really need to do is renovate. There are two methods of field renovation: till or no-till. I can either plow up the fields or poison them with chemicals. Either way, I need to eradicate the established stand so I can reseed.

By turning the sod under, then disking and cultipacking the ground, I can create a fresh seedbed on which to germinate the new crop. By using Roundup, or a similar herbicide, I can wipe out the vegetation but leave the sod untouched, whereupon I can plant the new crop with an implement called a seed drill. Both methods have their advantages and disadvantages. The chorus of advocacy, pro and con, grows strident as chemical manufacturers and environmentalists square off. Whichever way I look at it, mechanized farming is the culprit, but nobody talks about doing away with mechanized farming.

Plowing is time-consuming, and so burns up vast amounts of fossil fuel. Plowing brings up rocks, leaches the soil, contributes to bare ground washouts in heavy rain. Agricultural studies have shown that plowing also causes soil compaction, not only from the weight of the machinery, but also from the plowshare as it is pulled along, exerting downward pressure on the subsoil layer. Compaction of the subsoil hampers water absorption and thwarts the development of capillary roots. Repeated plowing can be responsible for dust bowls, field barrenness, and runoff depletion, and yet it is only the first phase of the renovation process. The additional procedures of disking (breaking up the overturned clods) and cultipacking (final smoothing) can aggravate the damage.

The no-till, chemical alternative to plowing is quickly accomplished and—according to every endorsement you read and hear—absolutely safe. The newer herbicides are reported to break down almost instantly into inert components that have no further effect on animal or plant life. A field can be sprayed, fertilized, and drilled in the same day. As the old crop withers, the new crop gathers strength to burst out of the ground. It sounds too good to be true. It *is* too good to be true. The drawbacks of chemical farming are not to be overlooked. Kill one thing, and two other things will spring up in its place. Underground, the quick fix becomes a lingering tragedy. Bacteria, worms, insects—everything gets wiped out when a field is killed. And repeated applications of herbicide are usually needed to do the job where the sod is thick, a fact I learn only when I take a moment to read the fine print.

Still, good burgher that I am, I weigh the choices carefully with respect to their comparative price. The delivery of herbicide on twenty acres (the approximate area to be renovated) plus the rental of a seed drill will cost a little over one thousand dollars. If I go the other route and equip myself with used tillage implements—a plow, a disk harrow, a cultipacker, and a PTO seeder—I will spend as much money, maybe more. I have already decided to re-plant the fields in timothy, the hay of preference for the horse owners who are the majority of my clientele, so the price of a couple hundred pounds of timothy seed is a given. To till or not to till, it is a tough call.

Ultimately, it boils down to a matter of trust. As convenient as they sound, I just can't bring myself to trust herbicides. Maybe it's my generation, maybe it's the Rachel Carson warning flag fluttering in my head. Promises of efficiency and harmlessness scare me. The well, our drinking water source, is at the edge of one field, and our vegetable garden is nearby. At field margins are wildflowers that mean as much to me as the hollyhocks and snapdragons Becky cultivates in the front yard. The pond is the collection basin for runoff from at least half the property; we not only stock it with fish, we stock it with ourselves in hot weather whenever the algae abates. If what they say is true, that farm chemicals are inert, why do I read in the newspaper that farming is a leading cancer-causing occupation?

I decide to renovate the hard way. Summer is over, but my tractors will not stand idle in the barn. Armed with the forethought that tedious hours in the tractor seat are soon to be added to my already busy schedule, I return to the venues of used farming equipment. I'm in the buying mode again. I'm looking for a two-bottom, sixteen-inch, three point hook-up, moldboard plow that'll fit the Oliver. With forty-two horsepower, two bottoms, or plowshares, are the maximum I'll be able to pull in this shale ground. I'm told that in the deep, loamy soils of the Midwest, six- and even eight-bottom plows can be yanked through with ease.

As I search among rusty candidates, I learn the nomenclature of a moldboard plow. Its backbone is a rigid frame, or beam, that connects the tractor to the two bottoms, one in advance of the other (and in this case, sixteen inches apart laterally). The pointed front of a plow bottom is called a share; extending above it is a cutting edge called a shank; and behind it, curving to overturn the earth that has been sliced through, the moldboard. On the other side of the moldboard is the landslide, a wedge that separates the furrows. Ahead of the share on a modern plow is a coulter wheel that rolls along like a pizza cutter, making the first incision in the ground, thereby reducing the drag on the share and the shank (both share and shank are primary wear parts). Fastened to the trailing edge of the moldboard can be trash turners, flanges that extend the moldboard curvature to ensure the complete flipping of grassy sod. To the rear of the hindmost moldboard can also be an iron wheel that trails in the furrow, thus helping to keep the plow correctly aligned despite the side pressure as it moves along.

In the buying and selling of farm equipment, I am an old hand by now. It doesn't take me long to find a plow that has all the bells and whistles. The International 420 I settle on even has trip bottoms, a feature that allows either bottom to break away backward, then reset, if a share point should snag in rock. The shares and shanks on this plow have many more acres ahead than behind. Although the red painted beam is muted to a weathered rose, every decal is intact. I have found the proverbial sedan driven by a little old lady to church on Sundays (according to the salesperson, the plow's previous owner used it once a year to turn a garden). The implement emanates the suasion of a good deal. I part with half of my thousand-dollar budget for half a thousand pounds of metal.

Plowing is the most elemental of all farming procedures. To rearrange the earth, even by hydraulic controls and the force of an internal combustion engine, liberates sentiments of husbandry that seem to be rooted in a primal substrata of the brain. The work goes slowly, so there is plenty of time to free-associate. Plowing is a systematic procedure, done in rows, accomplished by degrees. As I smell the freshly exposed ground, a sensation similar to intimacy hangs in the air. The earth and I are alone together. Plowing is like sexual intercourse—the literary allusion is well established—but there is more to it. The way the plow bottoms rip into the sod, displacing it then turning it upside down in two parallel taupe ribbons, is also like *thinking*. When the mental process is brought to bear on a problem, we scratch the surface of our consciousness and turn up what's underneath. We are constantly plowing old thoughts under. The furrows on our brows are indicative of the tillage within. To bring forth reason, to be inquisitive and examinational, is to leave no stone unturned.

Instead of maintaining my firm grip on the tractor's steering wheel, I could be grasping the handles of a one-horse plow—an Oliver Chilled Plow—and scarring a sagebrush plain on a prairie afternoon. The dull clank as share and shank strike obstacles in the soil is an archetypal sound, going back to the Age of Bronze, I suppose, when the sun-baked Mesopotamian plain was hacked at with primitive hoes. I am reminded of my father's labor-intensive ground breaking for the one or two vegetable gardens he planted during our years in Rhode Island (this was before he discovered the campus produce market). He spaded up the hard ground, directing the shovel blade as perpendicularly as possible and jumping on it with both feet for emphasis. One adjacent clump after another was overturned this way. It took him all day to do about a ten-foot square and it put him in a foul humor. To witness his anger made me angry, too. It was the most vexing thing I had ever seen—a grown man jumping repeatedly on a shovel, exhausting himself and exhausting me as I stood there watching him. Even at my tender age, I knew something about plows and harrows and tillers. I could have told him a thing or two. His energy represented a fraction of one horsepower—this college professor, this city-bred gardener—and he was growing testier by the minute. There was no point in offering to help him either, because I didn't weigh enough to drive the shovel point more than an inch or two by his method. Believe me, I had tried, and all I got was bruised arches.

The throaty chorus of the tractor's forty-two horses brings me back to the present. When pulling a plow, it's important to keep the rpm's up. As the two bottoms wedge through denser hardpan, the Oliver's engine automatically reacts; its throttle governor compensates for the sudden load with a fulminating enrichment of fuel. Within the cast-iron engine block, both harness and stable, petroleum-pampered steeds strain.

After creating the first double turning of soil on opposite sides of the field, I lower the tractor's right wheels into the empty furrow so that they are tracking ten inches lower than the left ones. This share rut, soon to be filled with overturned sod from the next pass, is the guide that enables me to keep subsequent furrows aligned. Aslant, I crawl along, scraping two hard-prized humps of overturned dirt and grass sixteen inches to the right. There's no way to speed things up; shifting to the next highest gear as an experiment, I only succeed in stalling the tractor. The tractor itself has a tendency to go sideways in reaction to the side-pressure on the moldboard. A straight line is steered when the tractor's front wheels are cocked slightly to the left, with a smidgen of brake drag on the right rear wheel.

It takes strenuous concentration for a beginner to do all this correctly along the first few furrows, but after I've plowed for an hour or two, my feet and hands are performing their tasks without conscious direction. Loosed, my mind considers the land as it must have appeared decades earlier, when it was cropped for corn, barley, wheat. I try to imagine what it was like to walk behind a mule—that power plant on hooves traditionally associated with forty acres. In terms of control, the one-mule-power plow must have been the forerunner of the airplane; it took a joystick sense of maneuverability to keep a furrow even and straight. Yet we think of plowboys as the crudest of farm laborers—the professional equivalent of hod carriers, sandhogs, deck-hands. Plowboys were the picaresque fools of literature who avoided the convolutions of the examined life and died young. And in truth, when I plow, I don't identify with airplane pilots.

Plowing is a hieratic task. To ready the earth for seed is about as basic as work gets, and if it's kept up long enough, sacred currents materialize in the sluiceways of the mind. It takes me nearly seventy hours (in three- and four-hour increments) to plow up twenty odd-shaped acres, and each day when I knock off, I'm reflective as hell. I feel as though I've communed directly with the spirits in the ground. Unseen by me, stray minié balls must be lying overturned, and arrowheads, too. The passage of previous centuries and cultures weighs heavily on my thoughts.

Quite obviously, I've been rearranging the very wellspring of life—the interface of soil and sunlight. By authoring the music of the plow bottoms as they scraped along, I contributed to the cyclical dance of renewal, that great spiraling amplitude of weed and manna. Gé, Earth, mother of us all—I am at her bosom. She has suckled me, so I must repay her in kind. I will kindle the fires of photosynthesis so that they rage verdantly through another growing span. I have plowed myself silly. I am preserving these fields the old-fashioned way, and in doing so, I am avoiding the easier, technocratic solution: the chemical swift kick that sends a plot of land back to winter in any season. Now I can only kick myself for embarking on this wearying, self-soliloquizing journey.

TWELVE

I NEVER WENT TO MONTCLAIR HIGH SCHOOL. My parents intervened, thinking that I was embarked on the path to juvenile delinquency – an altogether unwarranted conclusion with no supporting evidence, but one they reached because they couldn't understand my nominal teenage rebelliousness. Media idols were threatening their sway. Rock 'n' roll insulted their intelligence. Television, the newest household appliance, had become the devil incarnate, a filcher of family values. Clotheswasher, dishwasher, brain-washer. My parents rigorously monitored its use. "Perry Mason" was permissible (my mother's heart throbbed none-too-secretly for Raymond Burr), but shows like "Dobie Gillis" and "Peter Gunn" were considered subversive. The corporate exploitation of teenagers was a relatively new phenomenon, one my parents scorned vehemently. From my parents' pre–World War II standpoint, the years between childhood and adulthood were best passed in quiet study – or in wage-earning employment. To an insulting degree, I was minimizing both.

They enrolled me against my wishes in an all-boys preparatory school in Newark, a twenty-minute commute on the Lackawanna line in the company of attaché- and umbrella-toting adult white males. My brother, two grades behind, was enrolled as well, ostensibly to ensure a big brother–little brother buddy system, though we took great pains to avoid each other, not the least by choosing different seats on the train. My sister was exempted from the prep school mandate because she was attending a high school for gifted children at Montclair State Teacher's College (my brother's and my applications had been turned down).

When my mother and father announced their decision, I was stunned. Not only had I not been consulted about the school change, I never dreamed that prep school would be an option, given the proclivities of two erstwhile sociology majors who had grown up in the Depression years. Newark Academy was an élite institution, mummified in its tradition. It was founded two years before the Declaration of Independence, and as such was the second-oldest continuously operating day school in the nation. Tuition cost a bundle. How could a poorly paid college professor (if I was to believe what I had been told all these years) afford to send a son, much less two sons, to such a place?

The explanation was this: my maternal grandmother and step-grandfather had recently passed away, leaving my mother a modest cash inheritance. Once again, the wheels of educational betterment began turning in my mother's mind, and by coincidence, Newark Academy was embarking on a publicized expansion of its enrollment. For the first time ever, the Academy was actually seeking out students from diverse backgrounds—a few poor boys, a foreign exchange student, even a token black. In the coming years, girls would gain entrance as well. My brother and I were offered scholarships in light of my father's low income, and this tipped the balance for my parents' decision.

The switch to private school severed my public school friendships almost overnight; I lost track of nearly everyone who continued on at Montclair High. Newark-bound on the Lackawanna train each morning, I pondered my loss, growing angry, even inconsolate because I felt so entrapped by "privilege." I had been ordered to take the opportunistic fork in the road, and like a dutiful son, I did what I was told. It was expected of me to complete three more years of schooling, then go to college, and that was that. The strictures of the family's good name and, above all, my eagerness to please my parents, quelled every real urge to rebel.

I must have entered Newark Academy as the most belittled and benighted student in its long history. According to my new teachers and classmates, I was substandard in every respect. I had the wrong haircut and used the wrong grooming gunk. I wore the wrong tie, the wrong shirt, the wrong sport coat (required), the wrong pants, the wrong belt, the wrong socks, and the wrong shoes. I came from the wrong town (Montclair had its own prep school, the equally snooty Montclair Academy, a sports rival), the wrong *side* of town, and my parents drove the wrong kind of car. (Not being a doctor, a dentist, a lawyer, or a business tycoon, my father was in the wrong profession, too.) I carried the wrong pens, the wrong pencils, the wrong notebooks, wrote the wrong words, spoke with the wrong people, said the wrong things in class, asked the wrong questions, and held the wrong opinions. In gym, I ran wrong, threw wrong, jumped wrong, and climbed wrong. I was the wrong age (too young for my class), the wrong height, the wrong weight, and had the wrong kind of pimples on my face. In short, I was wrong as wrong could be.

My peers were boys of wealth and good breeding, many of whom had been Academy students since first grade. They had grown to feel secure in the unwritten rules that circumscribed the school's code of conformity. They all dressed alike, acted alike, thought alike. They did not truck to newcomers. In the class of '61, the topmost circle of six or seven boys divided up sports captaincies, officerships, and every other position of influence. A few of the boys were so brilliantly well rounded that they were sports stars as well as straight-A students.

The first thing I learned about my new classmates was their encoded hierarchy—the cool, the not-so-cool, and the totally un-cool. Naturally, I fitted in somewhere south of the bottom. Cool at a northeastern prep school in the late 1950s was the apotheosis of the term. To exhibit impeccable behavior, i.e., *to be cool,* meant that a boy's mannerisms and languor had to dovetail in a goofy kind of detachment. Enthusiasm was permitted only on the playing field. For a newcomer to win acceptance, sports acumen and the kind of car he drove—or would soon drive—were the initial litmus tests. Since I possessed neither, in addition to all my other negative qualifications, I was classified as a schmuck. I had little chance of ever becoming cool.

The boys at Newark Academy preserved their school's heritage by being there, suffering the whims of a quirky teaching staff and bearing the brunt of tradition-steeped rules and regulations. The boys' parents, those check-writing givers of opportunity, were the ones who really kept the prep school alive by perpetuating the myth of a quality education. For nearly two centuries, the school had instilled the values that would eventually pay off in the corridors of power and greed. Newark Academy's emblematic figure was the Minuteman: the long-legged, musket-toting, tricorn-hatted youth that strode across the school seal. The Academy building (its third) stood at one corner of a fenced-in athletic field next to the above-ground tracks of the Newark City Subway. Built in the 1920s, the school was a two-story, L-shaped, neocolonial brick structure with a white cupola on its roof. In its attic was a rifle range, and in its basement was a fencing parlor. Its classrooms bore the aging stigmata of slate and hardwood. Its science laboratory was brass-quaint. Its auditorium had a faded burgundy curtain across the stage and a tumultuous pipe organ that was exercised in morning chapel by a flaxen-haired gent who rolled his posterior around the organ bench as though he were on gimbals.

Along the tall confines of its gymnasium, where soot-ledged brick vied with wire-caged banks of windows, there was a permanent exhibition of extinct felt banners. An elapsed-time clock and a bulb-nubbled scoreboard warred from opposite walls. Ropes and rings hung down from the ceiling, trapeze bars folded out from nowhere, pull weights were racked perpendicularly to the floor. The basketball hoops were bolted to old-fashioned wooden backboards, seemingly braced for cannonballs. In one corner stood a parallel bar that looked like it might have doubled as a railway trestle. A maze of game boundaries had been painted on the maple floor, which gleamed dully from decades of shellac. The gym smelled sweetly of sweat and cleaning solvents. A set of dungeon stairs led down to the lockers and training rooms, and directly outdoors was that crunching, limed torture-way to which every gym class repaired for at least twenty minutes: the oval cinder track.

As a Third Former (boys in forms one through five were "upperclassmen," Fifth Form being the equivalent of high school's senior year) the looming of college was meant to be my overriding concern. I was there to prepare myself, as I was constantly reminded. Academy graduates routinely entered Ivy League, or top engineering schools, or the finest state universities. Getting there meant hard work and hard play, a philosophy that was spelled out in the promotional brochures, and so parents enrolled their sons and thought nothing of the expense, happy to pay for the opportunity that would beget future opportunities. And certain subjects were indeed stronger than in the public schools: math and English, for instance, and dead languages. Yet overall, the Academy's scholastic reputation — as I learned from three years in its classrooms — was overrated. Upperclassmen were exposed to all the right books — books that were considered advanced (at the time) for a high-school curriculum: the lesser known plays of Shakespeare, Boswell's *Life of Johnson*, the Federalist papers, Darwin's *On the Origin of Species*, and so forth — but sucking their marrow for the purpose of cramming for an exam was not the same thing as absorbing their qualitative essence, allowing the authors' ideas to enter the thought-stream. Newark Academy students were inured to the wonderment of art, because being cool meant turning a deaf ear to aesthetic sensitivity.

Besides, there was a serious discipline problem at the school. One measure of a boy's coolness was his ability to generate shenanigans in the classroom. My experience in nine grades of public school had not prepared me for what I witnessed: this was teacher-mocking elevated to an obsession. No teacher, no matter how *with it*, was spared this gleeful, hurtful baiting. A pedagogue's most obvious shortcoming was his vulnerable point (all upper-form teachers were male). Mr. Murps, the Latin teacher, had a stutter that was openly imitated in recitation. Bald-headed Mr. Jacobi, the history teacher, was referred to, to his face, as Mr. Jackoff. Mr. Skiffet, the aged librarian, muttered to himself and was echoed uproariously behind the stacks. When Mr. Évian, the French teacher, made attempts to disguise his hand tic by shooting his cuffs or fiddling with a textbook, his merciless charges rolled in the aisles.

An Academy classroom was also a proving ground for various clandestinely hurled projectiles. The trajectory of a piece of chalk, slung from the back row and ricocheting off a teacher's back as he wrote on the blackboard, occasioned room-wide mirth. Loop-de-loops of paper airplanes alleviated sonorous theorems. Erasers, pencils, notebooks—all these things flew freely and frequently, sometimes right out the open windows. In the least disciplined classes, the aerodynamic characteristics of anything that wasn't bolted to the floor were observed on a daily basis. When a teacher felt bedeviled enough to press for an admission of guilt by the perpetrator(s), his whole class turned mum. To threaten punishment to everyone in the room brought adenoidal choruses of denial. If a teacher persisted in meting out universal punishment, like a quiz or an extended session after school, he risked becoming the object of parental denouncement. To pit a teacher's word against a student's— in front of the headmaster—was usually a no-win situation for the teacher, a kangaroo court to exonerate the guilty party. (I see now, thirty years later, how demeaning this must have been, and I apologize for my complicity. I have no reason to preserve these unruly classrooms other than to hope that my children and grandchildren never find themselves in one.)

Almost every student cheated on exams. The attainment of passing grades was regarded as a communal effort. If you knew the answer to a question, you wrote it legibly in large script and then you bared your paper so your neighbors behind you and to the side of you could copy it down if necessary. Coughing the correct answer was another trick, one which was easy to get away with when everyone in the room contributed to the coughing fit. (It was cool to cough or sneeze cuss-words, too.) Writing answers on fingers, hands, wrists, cuffs, even trousers and shoe soles before an exam was de rigueur.

True creativity in cheating required a student to develop a two-faced attitude toward teachers, to be both brown-noser and back-stabber. It wasn't hard to outwit the pedagogues, many of whom were veterans of stricter and quieter eras of classroom comportment. The older the teacher, the more he suffered from a student's lack of respect. It wasn't unknown for a teacher to strike a bargain with a boy, offering an A for the suppression of bad behavior. One particularly pathetic appeaser had taught chemistry and biology at the Academy for forty years (he could remember some of his students' fathers). His hands trembled, his eyes had grown dim, but he stayed on the job because he loved it — an institution's institution. His biggest failing was that he couldn't turn his head and pivot his torso quickly anymore. Thievery in his laboratory was too easy; chemicals, or combinations thereof, that exploded or stank or fizzed or belched disappeared from locked cabinets *right under his nose*. To his boys, stealing was a lark, but when somebody tossed a sodium cube into a urinal, cracking the fixture and flooding the restroom (not to mention damaging the ceiling of the room below), he caught the blame. Nobody came forward to take the heat, and as a result, his remarkable teaching career was hastened to an abrupt end. In my vocabulary of oft-used exclamations, I still preserve two of his: "Well, all right!" and "I see no harm in that!"

The discipline problem was exacerbated by the headmaster and the assistant headmaster, who spent much of the day pussyfooting around the halls, attempting to nip trouble in the bud. Both were physically intimidating individuals who could glower with baleful authority when it was required of them, although the assistant headmaster, who was younger, prided himself on a kind of faked camaraderie with Fifth Formers. Both relied on a network of spies even as they made themselves out to be regular guys. Their deviousness was the perfect foil for the school's so-called code of honor. The way these two grown men dissembled and connived against the student body sent the message that successful lying would always be tolerated.

To be summoned (because of an infraction) to the headmaster's office was an opportunity to reiterate a lie, embellish it perhaps, but never recant. The darkly draped office was at the very center of the school, a door's knock from the anteroom where his much-ogled secretary, Miss Segal, worked. Miss Segal possessed the biggest breasts and the tightest sweaters in Christendom; many a boy willingly submitted to headmasterly interrogation just for the chance to stroll past her desk.

In his trophy-ornamented surround, the headmaster sat smoking his pipe and squinting through aromatic wreaths, poised to extract a confession. His method of inquisition was a combination of feints and probes, seemingly sidestepping the issue until the finger-pointing moment of accusation. As the occasional recipient of his roundabout questioning, I could never tell for sure when the knife-thrust would come – but I was prepared. I learned quickly that stonewalling was the great untaught subject at Newark Academy. Despite the incentives for confession ("No punishment this time, Svenson, if you tell me *exactly* what happened"), I was forged of stronger stuff. All I ever did was stick to my denial, knowing that I'd get off the hook on lack of evidence. Only the uncool turned to blubber in the headmaster's office.

A portion of each school day was taken up by study hall, where boys without a scheduled class bided their time in a central foyer presided over by an assistant football coach who sat at a desk on a podium with his feet up and his nose buried in the sports pages of the newspaper. His primary duty was to regulate trips to the restroom, which he did with a disinterested wave of his hand. Most students went to the restroom to smoke, a forbidden practice that risked discovery by the assistant headmaster, who often hid in the stalls.

Study hall would have been the ideal place for throwing things and "hacking around," for in it were parked the denizens of all five forms. Oddly enough, it was the quietest place in school. The very boringness of the period, its absolute waste of time, left nobody with the motivation to misbehave. Study hall was a no-man's-land in the battle between student and teacher, between student and subject matter. The most active thing in the room was the jumpy second hand on the wall clock. It was a drowsing period for some, and a studying period (I guess) for others, but for me it was a time to daydream.

I'd sit there with my unfinished homework spread across the narrow desk, absentmindedly twirling a pencil. I'd be thinking about Montclair High School, and the dances and football games I was missing. I'd think about Katie, who lived four doors down from us on Prospect Terrace. Katie was the eldest daughter of a vivacious family that saw everything and did everything our family didn't. She had been a grade behind me at Hillside, an always-smiling, curly-headed girl who seemed interested enough in me, though far too in demand to give me a soul mate's exclusivity. I saw so few girls these days that she was my girlfriend by a process of elimination. I needed to work up the nerve to invite her to the school prom.

On the pretext of using the pencil sharpener, I'd go to the window and stare out at the parking lot. Late-model T-birds, Impalas, Austin

Healeys, and MG's baked in the sun, cherished chariots of the lucky Fourth and Fifth Formers. The boys from the wealthiest families were given the car of their dreams when they turned seventeen, and the way they wheeled into the parking lot at 8:45 in the morning—top down, sunglasses on, necktie flapping over a shoulder—made me ache with envy. I would be the last person in my class to get a driver's license, an embarrassment of no small dimension. Being the baby of the form had absolutely no advantage; resolutely, I lived with the consequences— lining up rides, borrowing backseats. But I'd have been doubly embarrassed if I parked my parents' car in the school lot. Our '51 Merc sedan (the Kaiser's replacement) with its orotund contours and split windshield and advanced case of rust on its grille and bumpers would be more than an eyesore—it would be a laughingstock I'd never live down.

So for three years I endured the psychological hardships of what originally seemed to be a bad dream. I can't say I thrived in the atmosphere of privilege, but I embraced it the best I could. To be accepted as one of the guys was my overriding concern. Nobody in the history of the human race ever strove harder to be just like everybody else. It was a matter of survival. My adolescent self-consciousness and a growing shrewdness of mind had taken control. By degrees, I donned the protective camouflage of the Minuteman and partook of the cool, mid-century charade that masked the tender-hearted outsider, the boy who used to study trees in Rhode Island.

I became the next best thing to a ringleader, the runner-up who instigated pranks and urged others to join in—the point man. With purloined chemicals, it was I who made gunpowder that was used in the homemade torpedoes that would sink the rowboats at Branch Brook Park during the class picnic (fortunately or unfortunately, the torpedoes malfunctioned). It was I who re-drew Sparky, the cartoon dalmatian on the fire prevention poster, so that he resembled a canine demon from hell, fanning the flames. It was I who threw the first blackboard eraser. (Chalk-printing a teacher's suit jacket was a sure-fire method of earning classmates' respect.) It was I who elevated cheating to an art form.

And it was I who organized, by my third and final year, a palpable hierarchy of insidership for the senior class. Utilizing the same criteria that had put me at such a disadvantage when I first entered the school, I divided the Fifth Form into three ranks: the Élite, the Bourgeoisie, and the Rabble. It was a subjective pigeonholing, a quantification of cool, and it caught on like wildfire. Evaluation for coolness became the rage; Third and Fourth Formers imitated the idea immediately. My tripartite distinction was discussed by teachers and administrators, both of whom were warily impressed (I had taken care to peddle it as a sociological experiment).

Blurbs beneath the seniors' mug shots in the *Polymnian* – our yearbook, of which I was a staff member – assign each boy to a classification. Élite-hood was bestowed upon me and seven or eight others out of a class of forty. My portrait in black and white stares out at me today, and I am disconcerted by my bland seventeen-year-old face. I have just the right haircut. The hint of a leer intrudes on my smile as I stare into the camera; I'm oozing the casual self-confidence that Élites are supposed to ooze. The knot of a black knit tie is the centerpiece of my button-down collar. My blazer exudes a worthy provenance. I have no doubt that if the photograph were extended below mid-chest level, it would show my pressed chino slacks, my white crew socks, my scuffed oxblood loafers. I am a billboard of sartorial correctness.

The blurb beneath my picture does not go into the details about how I applied to Princeton and was rejected – a parting shot from the headmaster, whose recommendation could have gotten me in – or how I applied to Brown and suffered a similar fate. The blurb does not describe the high marks I scored on the college boards, or my determination to succeed in English VI (creative writing) despite my predilection for being a distinguished troublemaker. Nor does the blurb mention the emptiness I felt as my high-school days were coming to an end, or my trepidation at the advent of college in a third-choice school, or the guilt I was beginning to accumulate because of the stains wrought on my character.

No, it mentions only the following: I was an "outstanding Élite." I was the "Casanova" of the intercity bus line, having spent a snowbound Saturday night and Sunday morning with Katie somewhere between the Lincoln Tunnel and Secaucus on the last bus out of New York City. (The experience cemented our relationship but unglued our worried parents, who thought we had eloped.) I was the "star" of English VI. I was "regularly kicked out" of the school library (a nervy distinction for a person who worked part-time in a municipal library throughout his high-school years). I was a stalwart "member of the swim team and the track team" during a losing season.

The words were calculated to say just enough to convey an unmistakable aura of cool. The mystery of my persona hovered between the lines, so that fables could be woven in the warp of print. Magnified, even glorified I became, fodder for the reader's imagination. Some guy, this Svenson! Athlete, scholar, lover, prankster, blueblood! I wrote the copy myself.

105

THIRTEEN

P LOWING LEAVES RUGGED BROWN STRIPS, and then whole patchworks on the undulating quilt of well-thatched farmland. I do not unhitch the plow until mid-December, and when I do, I survey the turned-under acreage with a swelling sense of accomplishment. With my brute will – and the Oliver's brute strength – I have tamed the land. But by January and February (it is a snowless winter), the areas that have been plowed look so desolate, I begin to wonder if I'll ever be able to return the fields to their former productivity. I feel guilty for having made such a mess. Where I plowed deeply, shale rocks are strewn around, some as big as books; where I plowed thinly, the fescue is reasserting itself between furrows. Surely, my efforts rate only a B – , maybe a C + .

But I've only gotten started. The next step is to break up the overturned ridges and clods with a disk harrow, but the fields are too wet to work and I haven't acquired a harrow, although I am actively searching.

Disk harrows come in many sizes and configurations. Their principle is plain: a weighted gang of concave steel disk blades is pulled at an angle over the ground. The disks slice through the soil, ripping and redistributing it as they pass, leveling humps, filling furrows. The smallest harrows – the ones carried on a tractor's three-point hitch – have two short gangs of disks set in a V-formation at a fixed angle. These are fine for gardens and very small farms. The larger and more effective towed harrows have four gangs of disks in two V-formations, one behind the other, and their cutting angle is adjustable. Set to roll perfectly straight (for light disking and transportation), the disk gangs are parallel; set at their most oblique angle, the gangs form a ground-gouging X. The advantage of the four-gang configuration, or X, is that the front two gangs turn the soil outward, while the rear gangs turn it back in. This way, the soil is not actually displaced as the field is churned up.

A standard, four-gang towed harrow is a heavy implement, multi-jointed so that it can be pulled over uneven ground and turned sharply at field corners. Its biggest drawback is that it can't be towed on a paved road. The disks will scar the road surface and the pavement will dull the disk blades. There is a noise factor to contend with, too. A disk harrow rolling on asphalt resounds like a choir of banshees. The largest, most modern harrows—called transport harrows—solve this problem with a set of pneumatic wheels that can be lowered hydraulically so that they raise the entire disk frame off the ground.

I mention this because my biggest concern, once I find a harrow, is getting it home. Transport harrows are out of my price and horsepower range. The towed harrow I'm looking for is a forty- to fifty-year-old relic, roughly the vintage of the little red plastic one I hitched to my toy tractor in first grade. Driving the back roads, I've seen one or two. No longer mainstays in farm equipment fleets, the old pull-alongs become objects of rust, notorious for their immobility, most often found at the edges of overgrown fields.

As luck would have it, I locate such a harrow at an equipment dispersal auction in the rural northwest corner of Rockingham County. In a row of contemporary, pressure-washed farm implements, including several up-to-date transport harrows, the antiquated four-ganger stands out, a low-slung jumble of lichen-decorated iron. Some hard-up farmer winched it onto a flatbed and trucked it in from where it sat, perhaps for twenty years, to make a few extra bucks. It has no shiny metal anywhere (the most obvious indicator of recent use) except in the hitch pin hole at the end of the tongue. Beneath its rust and scabrous colonies, there is evidence of the abrasion of many planting seasons. On the front gangs, the disk blades have shrunk from dinner-platter to tea-saucer diameter. A few of the blades are cracked or egg-shaped, although none is missing. The pinnings and linkages between the gangs are similarly worn (I can almost hear the clanking yank of bygone tractors); still, they're all intact. I can't tell for sure what make or model the harrow is, but an old-timer who sees me down on my hands and knees in close scrutiny informs me that it's an Oliver PA-7, from the 1950s. I'm unconvinced. If he's so sure it's an Oliver, why isn't there a trace of green paint anywhere—on the underside of an angle bracket, for instance?

He chuckles at my ignorance. Didn't I know that many of the PA-7s were orange?

I had no idea, I reply. Did the factory run out of green paint?

But he ignores my query. "Look!" he says, tapping his cane-end at a riveted junction. Sure enough, between the greenish-gray lichens, there are minute enclaves of pinkish peach—the Oliver pedigree poking through in an unexpected hue. My interest intensifies. I *have* to have the old thing.

My possession is, to all practical purposes, a *fait accompli*. When the auctioneer comes along the ranks and opens the bidding, the gaggle of farmers is unseemly inert. *A hunnert dollars, who'll give a hunnert for this fine old harra?* In the silence of a few seconds, he's down to seventy-five, then fifty, then forty, thirty, twenty-five. It must be a vertiginous moment for an auctioneer—the free-fall before the first fool gives a nod. In a long pause such as this, it must seem like an absolute wasting of breath. I raise my bidding card out of human compassion. *Sold!* he crows, and calling out my card number to his scribe, he moves down the line, extolling the virtues of the next implement.

Nobody wanted the harrow, it is plain to see. And so I begin berating myself; if I had waited a second or two more, I could have gotten it for five, maybe ten dollars less. As scrap iron, it's worth every penny of that.

But I am preoccupied with the next task: getting the harrow on my pickup truck. Now that it is mine, I have the luxury of examining my purchase closer and finding more defects. There is welding to be done. The disk blades are in sorrier shape than I thought: both front gangs will need to be replaced, as well as numerous fasteners and spacers. I kick it, shake it, wiggle it, lift up one corner just to see how heavy it is. It must weigh close to a ton. With borrowed wrenches, I unfasten three stout bolts connecting the linkage between front and rear gangs. By halving the harrow, I hope it can somehow be heaved onto the pickup. I'll need assistance, but there's always a camaraderie at equipment auctions—it's customary for farmers to help each other load up.

I get the harrow loaded all right; four burly strangers come to my aid and together we shove the front, then the rear half aboard, but our efforts are not without deleterious results. My truck's tailgate gets bowed like a playing card and the cargo bed suffers multiple striations. That's what disk blades do best: they weigh down, they scratch. And after I transport the harrow home, even more damage is effected when I try to get it *off* the truck. I am alone this time, resourceful as a hermit. It takes a heart-pounding struggle to inch the two gang sets back far enough so that they tip groundward. Resting at this juncture, I have a sudden brainstorm. I climb in the cab and gun the engine, lurching the truck forward and free. The harrow halves crash hard upon the drive-way. The truck has aged five years.

Weeks later—after a lengthy refurbishment and reassembly—I am towing the old harrow through a plowed field. The unevenness of the earth makes for a jarring journey; although the tractor is moving slowly, I am very nearly jounced out of the seat. In order to smooth, I must ride roughly. With its front axle pivoting like a seesaw, the 550 lunges over the ridges, chugging to overcome the resistance of the disk blades, which are set at a moderate angle against the direction of travel. Tractor and implement rock along in slow motion, towboat and barge, across the metaphoric, swelling sea of a Shenandoah Valley farm. I caress the earth with iron, and the field succumbs in spirals.

As I loved plowing, so I love disking. To soothe the roughened ground this way is mesmerizing. Having wrung it topsy-turvy with the two-bottom plow, I am making it aright. Over my shoulder, I watch the clods disintegrate in a seven-foot-wide trail that begins to approach the friability of a seedbed. From fence line to fence line, each new pass is a invitation for anything green to grow. Continuing round and around the field imparts the surety of stewardship. It is a sensation worth pre-serving, this systematic, farmerly progression—so different from work-ing on a painting. When I put the brushes down, I'm in the throes of doubt, but when I climb off the tractor, I'm rock-solid with certitude. I *know* I've accomplished something. My sense of gratification isn't con-tingent on the vagaries of aesthetic self-evaluation. Maybe that's why farmers, as a rule, don't paint.

After my first and second trip over the whole field, I re-adjust the lever that sets the disks at an even greater angle, and the tractor is shifted to the next highest gear. I'm no longer concerned about driving over a sud-den gulch or hillock that will unhorse me or unhand my steering wheel. More relaxed now, I glance back and watch the plumes of soil as they are churned by the half-buried disk blades. A piquant, earthy odor rises from beneath the tractor, a scent that combines with engine exhaust and cannot be expropriated by word or image. Coursing through the bare dirt field, I am about to wrap up another step in the necessary procedure to turn it green again.

But before I can reseed, there is another implement I need to acquire. This is a cultipacker-pulverizer, a wide gang of side-by-side rollers that serves as a final smoother of the seedbed. Its weight pushes down rocks and firms the soil surface in a ridged pattern to promote seed growth and minimize runoff erosion. Once the seed is sowed or drilled, the cultipacker-pulverizer—or packer, for short—can be rolled over the ground again to enhance seed/soil contact. The faster the new crop sprouts, the less susceptible it is to damage and depredation.

The towed axleful of independently rotating, flanged rollers (sometimes separated by toothed sprockets that help bury rocks) is as simple an implement as one is likely to find on a farm nowadays. It is often used in conjunction with a drag—a log, a plank, a bush—for further effect. The very latest packers are multi-ganged, twelve feet or more in width, and some are fitted with secondary chisel shanks or disk blades; like transport harrows, they come with pneumatic tires for road travel. These expensive implements are responsible for the vanishing-point-flat, picture-perfect seedbeds on the covers of farming magazines.

Unfortunately, many farms that boast such scenes are the very ones that go bankrupt from uncontrolled capital expenditure. What the magazine covers don't show are the For Sale signs. Part of the problem is the farmers' addiction to bigger and better equipment. The cash flow is usually no match to the debt deluge. Despite my all-American predilection for spending unpocketed money, I have no wish to become a contributor to this predicament. And so I am looking for a small, used, single-gang packer (about eight feet wide), and I find one for a couple hundred dollars.

Then once again I am rolling the tractor over the fields, towing the packer (this time I purchased it from an equipment dealer who insisted on delivering it himself, thus sparing my truck further abuse) as I envision acres of green. The signs of early spring are everywhere now: in the russet buds at the extremities of branches, in birdsong, in the warmth of late afternoon, in the hum of machinery from neighboring farms. The ground is almost the way I want it, clod-free and yielding, and the bar-lug imprint of the Oliver's rear tires is momentarily incised before the follow-up obliteration. In my wake, I have corrugated the earth.

When I'm done, I earmark another couple hundred dollars of hay profits for still another piece of equipment: a PTO-driven seed broadcaster that sits on the three-point hitch. Plowing back the profits, it is called. More accurately, my behavior could be described as a refusal to do things the simple way. I am machinery dependent. As I plan ahead, I see no cutting back. I remind myself that I already own a hand-cranked broadcaster, the one with the red nylon bag that fits against my chest, the one I used on the former fence lines. It would not be an impossible task, to walk over twenty acres seeding by hand. In the old days, that's how it was done, and in the *old*, old days the sower dipped his or her fingers in a shoulder sack, cuffing the seed to the wind. I could re-enact Jean-François Millet's painting that has been reproduced a zillion times. I could farm as a figure from art history, a pantalooned peasant in front of a luminous sunset.

But I am enthralled by efficiency, by uniformity, and above all, by speed. Tractor-borne, I see myself doing a better job. It takes no feat of rationalization to justify a better job. At this stage of my farming career, I'm like every other farmer I know. I have not arrived at an equipment plateau. I won't even entertain the idea that I criss-cross a field on my own two feet. And for once I dispense with the niceties of scouring the countryside for a used machine. I'm burned out on that approach, too. Instead, I drive to town to an implement dealer, the same one that sold me the Oliver tractor, and pay cash for a new Garber seeder, a lightweight and overpriced forest-green box with an oscillating grate and a spinner on the bottom of it. It is a bigger, rigid version of the handcranked model. In its hopper, two fifty-pound bags of seed can be dumped, and on one side there is a regulating handle for the aperture that controls the rate of dispersal.

The standard broadcast for seeding timothy is twelve to fourteen pounds per acre. I follow this rule to the letter, adjusting the aperture to the correct setting, but from the Kubota's seat, it seems as though nothing is happening. The seed is so tiny, I can't see it as it is being flung into the air. This won't do. I need visual gratification at this point; it is imperative that I watch the seed fall to the ground. I widen the aperture slightly until I can just see a faint, fanning shimmer of tan. That's a little better. But gusts of wind carry away much of the seed, or so it appears. My careful plotting of consecutive passes, based on a theoretical broadcast width of fifteen feet, is useless; indeed, the tangibility the whole renovation process—completing pass after pass and being able to see immediate results—is suddenly negated. Empiricism having become a chimera, I can only see myself circumnavigating bare ground, steering an orange tractor with a green box on its rear, hewing to a queasy faith. I think I am doing the right thing, but I am not sure. I won't be sure until I see the first fine hairs of sprouting grass.

Days, weeks go by. I busy myself picking up the few remaining rocks that were half-buried by the packer but are now highlighted as a result of spring rains. I pitch the shale shot-puts past the field edges into the weedy realm where rocks don't matter. The fields are losing their fluffed, freshly cultivated aspect; with the settling of the soil, the ground takes on a barren, even repugnant cast. In the middle of the leached-out expanse, I get down on my knees to look for traces of sprouting. I'd be grateful for anything, even tiny weeds. I find nothing. Rivulets of erosion are establishing themselves on mini-slopes. Up close, the pulverized shale resembles gravel, and there are ferrous patches that imitate scattered shards of terra-cotta. Try as I might, I can't even distinguish a single timothy seed. The weather turns a little warmer, the sun gathers more of a kick, but the fields remain inert.

So this is crop failure, I muse. Over and over, I reflect on the things that might have gone wrong. I planted too early. I purchased bad seed. The seed blew away in the wind. The birds ate it. In a panic, I call the county agricultural extension agent. He confirms all the possibilities, but urges me to wait a little longer. I appreciate the advice, but because I am at the point of starting over again and desperate for some hint of success that would keep me from doing so, a rage of self-hatred ignites in my brain. How did I ever get into this business of farming? Why am I making hay? What makes an acolyte of art and music and literature become a devotee of tractors and farm implements? What is there to preserve if the creative genius goes so far astray? The painter, failed and frustrated, chooses not to rip up paper or canvas, but instead, acres of ground.

The brown fields mock me. I do my best to forget the whole plowing-disking-cultipacking-reseeding episode. I return to the studio with a vengeance, and for a canvas or two, my painting has a razor edge of emotion that is startling. I goad the colors, the brushstrokes, into furious compositions that seem to take substantive leaps in an unexplored direction. I see that I have not only preserved my ability to paint, but also given myself a new perspective.

One late morning after I have calloused my brush-holding fingers and fatigued my critical eye, I slip away from the easel for the purpose of taking a walk—just a mind-clearing, preprandial walk on a perfect spring day. I stride straight across the property to the cross-fence, which I scuttle under, belly-wise, so as not to snag my venerable studio sweatshirt on the barbed wire. And then I see what I have been longing for. A green fuzz tinges the brownscape.

FOURTEEN

W<small>HEN MY PARENTS AND</small> I <small>UNLOADED</small> my belongings on the curb outside Carmichael Hall at Tufts University, my coruscation of cool was melting into a nervous sweat. It was a warm afternoon in September 1961, and I had done most of the driving from New Jersey to the outskirts of Boston, but our route had grown complicated at its end with wrath-provoking wrong turns (my father had insisted on taking over the wheel after we left the highway).

As the Merc's trunk and rear seat were disgorged of my student necessities—clothing on hangers and in boxes, bedding, easy chair, desk lamp, typewriter, clock radio, cheap guitar—my parents disgorged themselves of last-minute advice. I was admonished to be frugal and studious as I carried armful after armful into the grim dormitory. The hallways of painted cinderblock, the overwaxed checkerboard of the tile floor made the place seem oppressive and institutional. To either side, birch veneer doors constellated with thumbtacks and bits of scotch tape opened onto two-person rooms that bespoke deprivation and plainness. Two beds, two desks, two doorless wardrobes, two windows. College was another word for prison.

The first week was devoted to a process known as freshman orientation, a series of lectures and informal meetings that every newcomer was required to attend. With a yarmulke-like beanie on my head, I was introduced to 1) a stuffed bull elephant on a dais in the geology hall, 2) the chanting of football fight songs, 3) encapsulizations of college history, 4) pep talks about school spirit, and 5) never-ending welcoming remarks. Everything was repeated for emphasis. At one point, the college president offered his personal condolences for my painful acceptance of adult responsibilities. As a member of that captive audience of summer-charged freshmen, I chafed at the folderol; I, for one, couldn't be filled to the brim with a sense of purpose. My enthusiasm sprang leaks. Tufts had been my third choice, my fallback school, and I was matriculated only because I had been rejected at other groves of academe, other elysian fields.

In all other aspects, though, my introduction to collegiate life went smoothly. I was blessed with a nice guy for a roommate, a chap from Connecticut named Bill. Not a harsh word was uttered between Bill and me, nor did we ever give each other cause for complaint or incompatibility. We remained on the level of friendly strangers, and it made for easy studying (we could ignore each other) and pleasant company in the dining hall and at freshman mixers, where our partnership helped both of us overcome the awkwardness of making conversation with members of the opposite sex. Bill hailed from a blue-collar background that set his upbringing in sharp contrast to mine. I was looking for girlfriends, but he was already looking for a wife. Bill had come to college to study accounting and economics; I had come because . . . well, I didn't really know why I was there, other than that it was expected of me. Bill was an inveterate study hound, a solid B student, while I cycled between A's and D's, always susceptible to diversion. Bill wasn't literary or artistic or musical in any way, while I couldn't sit still for five minutes without scratching another mosquito bite of creativity.

By itself, undergraduate life at Tufts could be self-sufficient, though somewhat insular. Situated atop a drumlin between the satellite cities of Medford and Somerville, the campus was ringed by a closely built, three-story neighborhood as middling as a white middle-class neighborhood could be. Within the locus of a block or two, it was possible to do a load of laundry, grab a bite to eat, hang out in a drugstore, and browse in a convenience store. But Tufts was only a twenty-minute ride by electric bus and trolley to the cultural riches of greater Boston. I quickly discovered the Museum of Fine Arts, the Isabella Stewart Gardener Museum, the Museum of Science, Symphony Hall, the Boston Public Library, and — on the nearer side of the Charles River — Harvard and Central Squares, where I could take advantage of the many tendrils of Harvard University. That's what I liked about Tufts: it was both space station and launching pad.

I had come to college with grand literary ambition. During my last year at Newark Academy, my English teacher had singled out my prose for frequent class discussion, an attention that caused me to blush in front of my rowdy peers but sharpened my powers of description. If I acquired anything worthwhile at Newark Academy, it was the confidence to write. Wordsmithing was like blacksmithing — the blank sheet of paper being my anvil, the pen my hammer. By the sweat of my brow, I crafted ductile, red-hot sentences by the barrowful. Having breezed through the college boards in English composition, I was ready for stiffer assignments. The summer after graduation was spent working on what I hoped would be a first novel, a fictionalization of my chemistry/biology instructor's demise. I invented some choice props: a murderous biology class, an equally intimidating cabal of teachers, a plot that hinted at a national security scandal, and a headmaster's nymphomaniacal daughter (who couldn't keep her hands off me). I even designed the book jacket—a little red schoolhouse with a slashing X crossing it out.

Needless to say, my jejune effort escaped notice, even though I was courageous enough to mail off the manuscript to a couple of publishers. My very first rejection slips seemed like labels from bottles of expensive wine, their typefaces and brevity indicative of palate-promising rewards. Authorship was attainable, but temporarily out of reach. The empty bottle syndrome. Please feel free to try again (and again and again). Yet it was the momentum of literary pursuit that propelled me beyond that otherwise indolent summer. In this one respect, I came to Tufts with high hopes: my writing ability was my ace in the hole. The powers-that-be would preserve and nurture a talent such as mine. I counted on being placed in an honors English program and exempted from that most pedestrian of liberal arts requirements: freshman English.

But when orientation week drew to a close, the printout of my class schedule negated that fatuous notion. I was assigned to English F, the section for functional illiterates. It was the lowest of low blows. Even Bill had been placed in a higher section, and his writing skills were on a par with a bad Japanese-to-English translation. Somebody had screwed up. It was not like me to be remonstrative, but this was an affront of the first order. I called on the head of the English department to demand an explanation and a reclassification. Tartly, she informed me that English F was where I would stay. I told her I deserved better.

"Little freshman scum," she said (maybe she didn't use those exact words, but her tone implied them), "you were placed in Section F as a result of our careful evaluation of your writing performance. We didn't put you there without good reason. Go to the class. Good day."

Her head ducked down to her more important desktop business and I took my leave, flushed with ire, craving my rightful due. I decided then and there to stick with English F just to show the bitch how wrong she was. The class was held at eight A.M. Mondays, Wednesdays, and Fridays in the ROTC building behind the steam plant at the bottom of "the

Hill"—location-wise, the fundament of the university. English department headquarters were in Packard Hall, an ivy-entwined bastion at the top center of campus, rightfully adjacent to the bookstore, and the *good* classes never began before ten, so the good students (and professors) had plenty of time to wake up.

The Section F instructor, Mr. Finkter, was annoyingly awake and alert at eight in the morning. In front of him, a sullen assortment of dullards, male and female, slouched in their chairs and answered only when called upon. Across the tableau of indolence, feet shuffled, faces yawned, books dropped. Paper cups perched on the chair arms issued wispy aromas (and frequent spills) of coffee. The radiators made obstreperous counterpoint with early morning catarrh. Class participation was something that had to be scraped off the floor.

Mr. Finkter wore the same bow tie and sport coat each morning, attire that began to look clownish as the weeks wore on. Short, pudgy, and pug-nosed with marcelled hair, he was a thoroughly unappetizing professor. His tortoiseshell bifocals imparted an owl-like approximation of wisdom. His voice projected a pouting discontent. Praise of text and students alike trickled thinly, while censure flowed out of all proportion, for belittling was Mr. Finkter's forte. At every opportunity, he berated the class as if to wake us up, lambasting a wrong answer and stitching his corrective diatribe with cutting remarks. He knew he was teaching a bunch of dummies, so why shouldn't he? Maybe next year or the next he'd be in charge of a more intelligent, late-morning section in Packard Hall. In the meanwhile, he was in the holding pen—a cattleman with a cattle prod.

As per the curriculum, we were assigned to write a series of Freshman Themes—thousand-word essays on various topics of Mr. Finkter's choosing—like "The Best Day of My Life" or "Why I Appreciate Nature." Tedious as these subjects were, I warmed to the task. Here was my chance to shine forth, to rise above the cess of mediocrity that surrounded me. Surely Mr. Finkter would recognize my worth! I dove into the platitudinous pond and came up with what I thought were original and elegant turns of phrase. The best day of my life was when I experienced satori while studying the peeling paint of a sunlit bulkhead on the Hoboken Ferry . . . I appreciated nature because nature appreciated me, an equation of mutual admiration . . . Heartfelt observations I chronicled, vignettes experimentally conceived, paragraphs that began with a twinge and ended with a twist.

I turned in my themes, expectant of appreciative A's, but Finkter, that little fucker, gave me F's. I one-eightied my style, and he gave me D's. I put myself in his shoes. He gave me C's. I quashed every attempt at originality and good taste, tossing off banalities like a tabloid scribbler, and he gave me B's. But no matter what I did, it never qualified for an A. Top marks belonged to top students, none of which inhabited this early morning bestiary.

The trying wore me down. If I indulged in a descriptive flight of fantasy, it was red-lined for unreadability. If I wrote a sentence without a verb, it was struck down as incomplete. If I used a word that sent a classmate to the dictionary, I was guilty of obfuscation. My carefully crafted pages of Eaton's Corasible Bond came back defaced with righteous scrawls: *This is not writing. This is not a word. You're not saying this correctly.* There was no pleasing Mr. Finkter. The more thought-provoking my compositions, the lower their grades. My plans for vaulting into the good graces of the English department were going up in smoke. There was no chance of nourishing the budding litterateur in me in the face of this opprobrium, which relentlessly chipped away at my self-esteem.

I squeaked out of that first semester in Section F with a C-minus, convinced of the hopelessness of majoring in English. My knock at the door of Packard Hall had gone unheeded. It behooved me to take a long, hard look at the other possibilities. At the time, Tufts had neither an art nor a music major to seek refuge in. I settled for a sampling of liberal arts classes, five a semester, to see what else might hold my interest. In the ongoing process of elimination, I ruled out mathematics (too difficult) and science (too dreary, although later I would take excellent courses in the geology department). I ruled out economics and history (too pedantic, too run-of-the-mill). I ruled out philosophy (Plato was a gas, but advanced courses seemed headed toward overly abstruse shoals), sociology (off limits), and psychology (the statistical swervings were stultifying—too many bell curves). I ruled out foreign languages (but I managed to take a smattering of French as well as three semesters of classical Greek).

Only one field of study remained: government. I became a government major. I had no particular aptitude for political science—in fact, I was making D's in the required freshman lecture, Introduction to Government—but it seemed like the path of least resistance, a major I would not have to get serious about.

The introductory lecture, Gov-101, was held in a chemistry amphitheater for lack of space. The professor, the departmental chairman who paced the narrow podium beside the gas jets and hose bibs that sprouted from the demonstration counter, was a rumpled, pipe-chewing holdover of 1940s debonair – three-piece suited with a boutonniere and an artfully combed helmet of silver hair. At his back was a yellowing Periodic Table of the Elements. He spoke in a singsong mumble about a science that needed no apparatus. His lecturing style was other-worldly, hypnotizing. All he did was talk and walk until the bell rang, brooking no input from his listeners. Teaching assistants did the dirty work: test-administering, grading, term-paper reading. He just discoursed like an automaton to the hundred and fifty of us who composed his thrice-weekly audience.

Sitting in the back row, I could tell he was a brilliant thinker, and I could catch his words if I strained hard enough, but his thoughts all ran together like watercolors on wet paper, and in the wash of his nonstop ideas it was difficult to figure out exactly what point he was making. Yet somehow this careless and copious dispensing of information impressed a malleable mind like my own. I changed my seat to be a little closer. I started to be attentive to what he had to say. Clearly, the professor was on top of his subject (he was an internationally recognized authority), and the jumble of knowledge he unloaded began to interest me. If this comprised the study of government, I would learn it.

Despite my poor grades, I continued to admire his peripatetic performance. Here was an educator who utilized his skills in a remarkable way – unburdening himself of everything he knew, whether his audience wanted to hear it or not. His interpretations of the history of governing bodies, from the earliest recorded time to the present, were really quite fascinating. He distinguished between monarchy, oligarchy, and democracy, and traced their separate evolutions. He differentiated the various -isms of the past and present centuries, suffixes that unleashed unprecedented human suffering on the world. My earlier tendency to daydream during his lectures was all but banished. I struggled to become an alert note taker.

It was the beginning of the 1960s and I was at the hub of the universe – as the American transcendentalists had referred to Boston – and in Kennedy country, to boot. I couldn't help but see my choice of majoring in government in a positive light. Perhaps it could be a stepping-stone to a career in diplomacy, and I could be the next Lawrence Durrell – attaché by day, novelist by night. In those heady years of Camelot, diplomacy was a class act. No college student in the Boston area was immune to the siren song of a better world. The Peace Corps was in place, the civil rights movement was off to a sitting start, the beat poets and

120

the dharma bums were downshifting from highbrow to funk. And through the fabric of socio-political change wove folk music's insistent threnodies of love and oppression and justice.

At some point I let go of my inclination toward an exclusionary focus of study. The department chairman's logorrheic flow had loosed my mooring lines from the would-be safe-haven of Packard Hall. Now that my imagination was being swept downstream, I would do myself and my country a favor. I settled into my chosen major, knowing that I could accomplish a secondary goal as well—the freedom to take pretty much any other college course I wanted to. As long as I passed one or two government classes a semester, I could build up enough major credits to graduate in four years. This would allow me to divide the rest of my credit hours between other disciplines. And yes, I could take advanced English courses—in literature and creative writing, for instance—without the hassle of being an English major. Tangentially, I could preserve my creativity, and be all the more well rounded for it.

FIFTEEN

O̲N A C̲O̲N̲F̲E̲D̲E̲R̲A̲T̲E̲ M̲O̲N̲U̲M̲E̲N̲T̲ at the Perryville Battlefield in central Kentucky, about a forty-five-minute drive southwest
of Lexington, a larger-than-life soldier made of marble slouches at parade
rest. He wears a broad-brimmed hat and his two hands grip the barrel
of his rifle. He is facing south. The plinth on which he stands is in a
walled-off enclosure where two large rectangular pits were dug to accommodate the corpses of more than 400 soldiers in the days following
the battle, which was fought on October 8, 1862. Erected in 1901, the
monument bears a list of officers and "444 unknown heroes," and below
this, a four-line inscription:

> Nor braver bled
> For a brighter land,
> Nor brighter land
> Had cause so grand.

When I first read these words, their freight of nuance hits me with
full force; I am bowled over with reflexive sympathy. Van and I have
driven to Lexington to attend a conference on the preservation of battlefields jointly sponsored by the National Parks Service and the Kentucky
Heritage Council. Now, with eighty other conferees, we are spilled out
of two tour buses at the historic site. It is the kind of June afternoon
that achieves meteorological perfection. It is a day for unplugging clocks,
ignoring wristwatches—a time to stretch the legs by walking to the horizon and back. Some people are viewing the cannon replicas, others are
perusing informational plaques, still others are visiting the restrooms.
Two University of Kentucky students dressed as soldiers—one Union,
the other Confederate—execute a pas de deux between the parking lot
and the Confederate memorial. The stage has been set for us; a Potem-

kin village by chance and design, a lucky Kentucky afternoon that will leave us all with a favorable impression. The Civil War lives, breathes.

The ride from Lexington along highways that border endless configurations of board fence (of the horse farms) has been impressive enough. Within the bus, the earsplitting conviviality periodically diminishes as we gape through the tinted windows. Our tour guide jokes that this is the only place in the world where there are more horses than people. "Y'all ever heard of So-and-so [a famous racehorse]? Over to your right, that's his farm!" It almost sounds as though the horses ride the people. Surely, an equestrian God with a big-toothed grin reigns over this patch of planet. The black, tarred barns and the fencing, not to mention the glossy steeds gamboling therein, make ordinary problems like overpopulation and poverty and pollution seem distant. This is the land of a tourist brochure, and we cruise through it like aliens from space, cocooned in air conditioning, anticipating the conversation-stopper at the next bend in the road.

Our tour guide softens us up history-wise as well. Pivoting to face us in his frontmost aisle seat, he booms into the spring-wired microphone the particulars of the Confederate plan to "free" Kentucky in 1862. Marching from Tennessee, the rebel forces of Generals Braxton Bragg and Edmund Kirby Smith invaded the state, acting on the belief that Kentuckians would rise up and embrace the Confederacy. Smith took the capital city of Frankfort on September 3, and Bragg, who had slipped around a Union army at Nashville, Tennessee, headed in the direction of Louisville. The Union army of Major General Don Carlos Buell raced to Louisville to prevent the capture of the Union supply base there. Buell got to Louisville in the nick of time; with a refitted and reinforced command, he was able to press Bragg as he moved into central Kentucky to join forces with Smith. On October 8, 40,000 men of Bragg's and Buell's armies clashed at Perryville, leaving more than 7,500 casualties. Although Bragg's Confederates were victorious by eleven P.M., at midnight he ordered a withdrawal toward Harrodsburg, nine miles to the north, to link up with Smith's army. Bragg had come to the sudden realization that he had been fighting only a small portion of the Union army, and in truth, most of the Federals, including Buell himself, had sat out the battle because of poor or nonexistent communication from the front. Buell had not even been aware that the battle was *taking place*. Bragg joined forces with Smith, but disregarded the wishes of his officers to re-engage Buell's full army, which the Confederates now handily outnumbered. Buell, for his part, allowed the Confederates to withdraw unmolested, and because of this—and his earlier mistake—he was relieved of command.

It is a thoroughly American drama, pregnant with cinematic possibilities. It is a hell of a way to kick off a conference. By the time we step out of the buses at Perryville, every one of us is redolent with the Civil War. And coming upon those four brief lines chiseled in stone, I feel as soupy as a vaseful of plastic flowers. There is a lump in my throat, a lachrymal welling I am only just able to hold back.

I write the lines down in my notebook, just to be sure I don't lose them. Under my breath I repeat them over and over in a mantra that summons loss and courage. By doing so, I am fleshing out the glory that was the Confederacy, I tell myself, but in the space of fifteen minutes— the time we are allotted to walk the historic site—I experience an unanticipated phenomenon: my appreciation wanes. Much as I admire the simplicity and conciseness of the quatrain, I am beginning to doubt its veracity. Now that I am analyzing its content, the sentiment isn't holding together. The alliterative veneer cannot hide the fact that something is dreadfully wrong. *I do not agree with a word of it.* The four lines suddenly strike me as being utter bullshit. Using my mental socket wrench, I take them apart. There are only three parts, really. This is what I do:

Nor braver bled. Soldiers are all alike everywhere, at all bellicose moments and junctures, from the earliest clashes of our hunting-gathering foreparents to the most recent bloodbaths in the so-called civilized world. On the average, a soldier is a follower of orders, a cog in a killing machine. Okay, I'll admit there have been soldiers of outstanding courage—people like Alexander, Caesar, Joan of Arc, Napoleon, Grant, Patton, Eisenhower, MacArthur, Ho Chi Minh. The list of Illustrious Warriors is many feet long in pica type. But think how long that list would be (miles and miles, perhaps) if it included everyone who ever fought in *every* army there ever was. I can't help but think that the *nor braver bled* refers to the common soldier—in this case, the sacrificial boy from the South. It is he who is sculpted in stone, here in Perryville and elsewhere.

What the first line tells us is that the average Confederate soldier—the casualty—was as brave as any soldier anywhere, or to put it another way, no soldier in any war was braver than he. I question this assumption because I don't think it's true. How can we entertain such an idea, considering the gamut of armed conflict throughout human history? In my opinion, saying that these Confederates were as brave as the bravest soldiers of all time is a flip oversimplification, a generic type-casting that clouds the issue. Many of the dead soldiers at Perryville may not have been brave. Bravery is not a mantle everyone can, or cares to, wear. Bravery is also a fluid thing: one moment we have it, the next moment we don't. If I happen to be just standing there and a bullet hits me, I haven't been brave in the least. Moreover, it's an affront to those soldiers who really were brave to say that everyone else was of a similar mind. But most disturbingly, the assumption that a fallen soldier was as brave as any soldier anywhere is to reduce to notion of bravery to an honorary but meaningless decoration, a Kentucky Colonelcy. If bravery means getting oneself killed, who but a suicide really wants to be brave?

In Kentucky in 1862, the majority of the population had no intention of being brave. Entering Kentucky, Generals Bragg and Smith brought wagonloads of muskets, anticipating the recruitment of the hordes of willing fighters who were itching to join the Southern Cause. They miscalculated badly. Few signed up. Few actually wanted to die. And so the linkage between bravery and death is suspect. Bravery is no excuse for being dead; conversely, dying in battle does not necessarily imply the manifestation of sterling character traits.

Nor brighter land. The Dixie syndrome is at work here: soul-stirring fifes and drums, silhouettes beneath the magnolias, grinning cotton pickers, aristocratic largesse. The South is portrayed as the flower of democracy, the noblest part of the nation; so noble, in fact, that it is looked upon by the rest of the world as a beacon in its quest for independence. In its brief existence, the Confederacy shone as no nation has before or since.

But is this true? Emphatically not! The use of the word "brighter" undoubtedly is meant to be synonymous with "promising." But if the South had such promise, as the poetaster infers, why did it offer so little promise to its citizens? Apart from the monied class, few in the South had much to gain by the defiant maintenance of the status quo. The slaves had no stake in a future designed to keep them in bondage. The white farmers and factory workers who were whipped up with militancy owed the brunt of their enthusiasm to regional and cultural kneejerking. Their benefits within a caste system overseen by the landed gentry were chimerical at best. It is a documented fact that the lower- and middle-class masses fighting the South's military battles did so with an increasing pessimism as the four years of war took their toll. There was no saving grace in the coming defeat.

So in reality, the Confederacy was a benighted land, not only in terms of its promise to its citizens, but also because of its moral and philosophical underpinnings. The gaily fluttering battle flag was a symbol that drew attention away from the rottenness at the core of national identity. By turning against the North, its economic superior and constitutionally designated partner, the South made apparent its long-unreconciled sense of inferiority. Ruminating on this, I am brought face to face with the fourth line of the quatrain on the monument: *Cause so grand.*

The underlying reason why North and South split so decisively, and ultimately so tragically, was the slavery issue. Yes, there was indignation, there was anger, there was the fracas over state's rights and a deep mistrust of Lincoln as he was about to make good his first election bid — but at the base of it all, the festering institution that made one person the property of another held sway. Contemporary scholars of American history agree that chattel slavery was the bottom line of the Southern Cause.

Before the war, there was nearly universal recognition of the abhorrence of slavery, although two very different timetables for its eradication had evolved. In the North, where slavery had already been outlawed, the abolitionists wanted to speed things up by forbidding the establishment of slavery in the new territories as states were added to the Union. In the South, where slavery had been rationalized as economically indispensable, the white ruling class wanted God to make the final decision (God was notorious for putting off decisions); in the meanwhile, the genteel Southerner claimed that indentured servitude offered African-Americans moral and intellectual instruction.

The Southern Cause's bogusly reasoned claptrap of gentility and racial domination was a poor camouflage for economic oppression. It was ascribed to by educated men and women who should have known better (that is, if they took the precepts of the Founding Fathers to heart). Tainted by this overlooking of evil, the Cause was nevertheless wrapped in worthiness and burnished with a patina of uprightness. Robert E. Lee's infamous decision, as a son of Virginia, to quit his colonelcy in the United States Army and accept the rank of general in the Confederate States Army was a prime example of soldierly probity. When a career soldier forswore his vow to defend the Constitution, it could be inferred that his honor was at stake. And however misdirected or misapplied Lee's notion of honor may have been, it was a notion of supreme, if not sublime importance. It was at once a personal and public statement. Not surprisingly, the rank and file were only too eager to follow suit.

The fictionalization of Lee's character — from whatever it really was to the wisdom-spilling, soft-spoken, healing presence that became a rote quantification for biographers and school children—is still with us as the twentieth century draws to a close. It is the last bastion of the American equivalent of chivalry. To my mind, this image of Lee and the Southern Cause are interchangeable, damnably so. Too many people believe the myth. Male offspring across the nation have been given Lee as a middle name (my own father, a New Jersey Yankee, for one). It's like saying the Confederacy wasn't such a bad idea after all. In its heyday, slavery may have been the major issue dividing the nation, but racism united the North American continent. Unhappily, it still does. Yesterday, Duke Ellington and his orchestra toured the country by rail, and in every city they played, they slept in a Pullman car on a siding because their adoring audiences denied them admittance to hotels. Today, urban African-Americans find themselves in a losing lottery with every statistic—crime, drugs, unemployment, mortality.

No, the Cause was not grand, not in the least. Rather, it was pinched and small-minded, filled with code words that we still hear from under candescent hoods with eyeholes that continue to burn with hate. It was an excuse for national waywardness, a provocation to craft lofty ideals from racist bunkum. At Perryville, the soldiers in the ground beneath the soldier on the pedestal, that stonecutter's approximation of flesh and blood, could have been given a better epitaph.

Are Confederate memorials worth preserving? Yes, of course they are. Is a seemingly inoffensive quatrain that turns out to be a loaded political pistol worthy of contemplation? Yes, of course it is. To learn the lessons of history, the language of hatred and hurt must be understood. Losing the war and mourning her losses, the South vowed never to forget. Whether or not we identify with the Cause, a cry of pain on a marble monument still deserves to be read.

SIXTEEN

BY THE START OF MY JUNIOR YEAR at Tufts, I had opted
to live off campus. The restrictions of dormitory life, its conformities
and annoyances, were counterproductive to my maintaining an even
keel. Through the luck of a draw, I had been assigned one of the coveted
single rooms in Carmichael Hall for sophomore year, but I noted scant
improvement. Less and less I found myself able to study with cinder-
block-filtered stereos tempting the periphery of my attention. Losing
sleep because of drunken hoots that reverberated along the corridor at
three o'clock in the morning made me grouchily philosophical. Why
was quietness held in such low esteem? Wasn't there a baseline of respect
for others, to which all people, raucous or retiring, adhered? And why
couldn't I have a girl in my room without obeying the asinine regulation
of wedging the door ajar with a towel?

In order to preserve my privacy, that stipulation of life I was beginning
to find indispensable, it was imperative that I move out of the dorm.
Looking around, I decided to rent a room on the third floor of a two-
family house on Teele Avenue, a few blocks from the Hill. The first and
second floors were inhabited, respectively, by a baby maker and a wife
beater, and their sulking spouses. I didn't necessarily find my new
quarters quieter than a dorm room, as I was now within earshot of
domestic altercations that frequently rose to gale force, but my new-
found sense of personal freedom made up for it. It no longer seemed as
though I were a rabbit in a warren, or a dove in a dovecote. I had a bona
fide street address, not a campus box number.

Moving off campus was considered a fairly enlightened, even bohe-
mian thing to do at Tufts in 1963. For a nineteen-year-old, it was also
a seminal foray into adulthood. In residence in the two other rooms on
the third floor were two upperclassmen—a native of Finland who
retreated into his collection of Sibelius whenever the woes of collegiate

life got him down (which was often) and the rebellious scion of a corporate magnate from Connecticut, whose countercultural posturing went straight down the stripe in the middle of the road, i.e., the shoulder-length hair, the army jacket, and the stricken look of dope and depression that announced to the world an antagonism that knew no bounds. He was fair and skinny, malnourished by choice; he roved the fringes of the civil rights movement, a Harvard Square demonstrator. In private, he confided to me that he wished he had been born black.

In the room that faced the backyard like my third floor bedroom in Montclair, I arranged my possessions on low shelves of cinder bricks and throwaway boards. My bed was a re-fumigated mattress from the Salvation Army, my desk was a door that bridged two sawhorses. Between bouts of studying, I found the time to begin another fictional opus—this one about a poetically consuming off campus romance to which I aspired in real life. The anesthetic of my aversion to freshman English had worn off. I had actually achieved a measure of success in two creative writing classes during my sophomore year; a sympathetic professor had been able to steer me back on course by showing me how to analyze the mechanics of good prose. With her encouragement, I submitted stories to *The Tuftonian*, the school's literary magazine. Much to my surprise, the stories were accepted. Finkter-free, my wordsmithing was functional again, and what's more, I was invited to join the staff of the magazine as a regular contributor. I was becoming that Lawrence Durrell live-alike of freshman fantasy—the distracted poli-sci trainee airily absorbed in a higher preoccupation: the written word in the native tongue.

I was doubly surprised, however, when at the end of my sophomore year I was nominated to be the next editor of *The Tuftonian*. I hadn't expected so much so soon, nor had I lobbied for the honor in any way. The editorship was clearly English majors' turf (and usually reserved for seniors), yet now it was offered to me, a lowly government major, carte blanche with the implicit approval of the English faculty. The literary world moved in mysterious ways. I accepted.

That first week of fall semester, coinciding with my ensconcement off campus, I settled into the new job. I was assigned an office—my very own office!—near the bus stop at the bottom of the hill, and given a budget and the latitude to publish the magazine any way I saw fit, as long as I didn't overspend. Pure freedom of the press, pure unalloyed freedom! This was the kind of responsibility I had only dreamed of. I felt like Johannes Gutenberg about to strike his first plate. I felt like young Ben pregnant with Poor Richard. Singlehandedly, I plastered the campus with posters, calling for a general meeting for all interested contributors.

On the appointed night, I was pumped up with the courage of a prophet. There amid the smoke and laughter, I proclaimed whatever relevancy popped into my head. We'd chart a new course for a college literary magazine, I told my curious audience. We'd showcase new talent, hear from new voices. Our goal was to bring the power of literature directly to the *people*. Enough of the élitist crap! Anybody could write! Literary excellence came from the barrel of every student's pen.

My ad-libbed phrases were very much in tune with the politics of change, otherwise known as the Student Movement. Everyone agreed that a grass-roots takeover of the stuffy institution was overdue. Everyone wanted a crack at being creative. The idea that *The Tuftonian* should be re-invented along the lines of the current political climate was certainly not original to me; my embodiment of vague precepts was a sign of the times. In all likelihood, any other student could have spouted a similar message calling for a flying start. I had read a little Marcuse and McLuhan, so like everyone else, I was on the picket line of faddish intangibles –in this case, the triumph of literary freedom over bookish oppression, or some such crusade. The clarion for activism could be applied to anything that resembled becalmed acquiescence to the status quo.

I knew we were on a roll when the submissions came pouring in. Poems, prose, artwork, even term papers and freshman themes dropped through the letter slot, the accumulating mound plowed like a snowbank against the wall every time I opened the door. It was both gratifying and exhilarating to sit at my desk with my feet propped amid the piles of paper. How omnipotently I sifted! All branches of the student body were contributing, even engineers and occupational therapists. I strove to avoid protracted second thoughts that would subvert the spontaneity of the editorial process. If a piece struck my fancy, I'd mark it with a red A for approval and pass it along to my assistants, two female English majors who'd haggle the merits between themselves. If a syzygy of opinion occurred, the piece went in the magazine.

The first issue of the new *Tuftonian* came out in mid-November, and it hit the campus like a breath of fresh air. The readership was immediately pleased to find so many four-letter words, but beyond that, it was supportive of the expanded size and scope of the publication. More contributors than ever before saw themselves in print for the first time (and a few regulars, members of the established literary clique, found themselves omitted). I had pretty much allowed my own talents free rein with drawings and poems, including a villanelle about Superman visiting a delicatessen. On the opening pages, I hogged the editorial space with a rambling manifesto, replete with made-up quotations. My zeal may have been excessive, but it was heartfelt, and for that reason, unabashedly contagious. Literary-wise, the whole campus seemed to be dancing in the streets.

And then Jack was killed in the motorcade in Dallas, and every person, every building, every tree seemed to go into a state of shock.

The university had no choice but to shut down early for Thanksgiving vacation. Teachers and students alike, we all just gave up. The news images that had compelled us to feel good about ourselves—despite that little scare in Cuba—were suddenly ghost images and after-images. The whole world had signed off. As a freshman, I had taped the magazine covers of Camelot to my wardrobe to scrutinize the comforting visages whenever I felt deficient in national pride or spirit. They were our king and queen, from a lineage of wealth and good looks, yet they succumbed to the tackiest, most senseless of denouements—victims of the slightly built man with the weak chin and warped mouth, who poked an outdated Italian rifle from the window of something called a book depository.

I'll never forget my ride on the MTA out to Logan Field to catch the Newark-bound shuttle. By bus, trolley, subway, then bus again I reached the airport among passengers who stood and sat in the most pained of private griefs. There was open weeping and occasional rhetorical remonstrance that the country had, indeed, gone to the dogs. Whatever stiff-lipped resolve other, living political leaders were furnishing over the airwaves, it was clear that a light had gone out. For the idealistic youth of America, in whose ranks I certainly belonged, life was to take on a cynicism that would not achieve amelioration, social or political, until the bloodletting of additional public assassinations and the wasteful war in Southeast Asia was over.

Returning to school at the close of the holiday, I witnessed the spate of memorials that filled several issues of the campus newspaper—spin-offs of the new literary consciousness I had helped to raise. I collected myself as best I could. My first duty was to preserve this populist, creative voicing. My classwork was shifted to automatic pilot (on which it remained, more or less, for the duration). As the nation's healing process continued, I busied myself with my writing, doubling and even trebling my output and encouraging others to do so as well. It was a period of shared reflection. Given the uncertainty of the moment, the slender deanery of Tufts literati might as well be fattened for posterity.

As spring semester got underway, the collecting and editing of submissions for the magazine began to reoccupy the brunt of my time. I was also involved in poetry readings, student plays, and assorted symposiums. In the campus literary milieu, I had become the great enabler. Moreover, my love life was undergoing a classic recidivism – part of the way, all the way, then none of the way, due to moral second thoughts that bloomed with the deflowering. Fortunately, I was slated to spend the summer in France as an exchange student in a work-study program, thus extricating myself from all binding relationships. But as preoccupied as I was in projects and amours, I failed to anticipate the trouble I was running into: censorship of *The Tuftonian*.

In retrospect, I give the dean of students credit. If there ever was a felicitous moment for a crackdown, this was it. The surge of free expression, followed by the tragedy that shook the underpinnings of society – what better moment to dispatch the shock troops? At issue was a poem a friend of mine submitted, a vers libre about a spurned lover lying alone and playing with himself that included two very ordinary words: *penis* and *masturbate*. It never occurred to me that the terms might cause offense, but then I understood. The two words were a pretext for general displeasure; the Tufts administration was venting its disapproval of the previous issue of the magazine. Re-imposition of faculty control over *The Tuftonian*'s contents was what was really at stake.

Summoned to the dean's office, I was shown the typewritten page of manuscript that had mysteriously disappeared from my own office several days earlier. There followed a low-keyed, but firm dressing down. It was entirely out of the question for me to consider a poem like this for publication, the dean said. It was bad form.

His pipe-clenched words brought me to a boil. Usually I was a calm recipient of criticism, but something in the headmasterly tone of his voice tripped my release-wire.

How, I wanted to know, had he gotten hold of the poem? It had been "submitted" to him, he said. By whom? I asked. By a faculty member, he said. So that was who! That weenie what's-his-name, in his cubicle upstairs in Packard Hall, the one who was listed on the magazine's masthead as Faculty Advisor – a phony position if there ever was one, for he had never advised me about anything. It was he who had ratted! The quisling! Come to think of it, his vapid presence *had* been noted at one or two recent editorial meetings.

I tried my high-handed approach. *The Tuftonian* was a student-run publication, I reminded the dean. As long as I was editor, I answered to nobody. A toady in cahoots with the administration had no right to be included in the editorial decision making. It was a tampering with the process of free expression, it was un-American. I demanded the faculty advisor's dismissal and an apology. And I wanted the poem back.

But the dean was unmoved by my theatrics. Removing the meerschaum from his mouth and fixing me with a level gaze, he informed me that I could be kicked out of school for insubordination, and that he personally would not hesitate to do it. I had a responsibility to preserve the good name of the university. Some words and ideas were just not literary (here I burst out laughing). What he meant was that a campus magazine should not read like a D. H. Lawrence novel. Or one of those trashy Henry Miller things. After all, he continued, there were so many other tropics, er, *topics* to write about besides sex. What about science fiction, this business of sending a rocket to the moon? What about old-fashioned heroes and heroines? Not everyone was as, ahem, *advanced* as I wanted them to be (here I tried to laugh but I couldn't). Certain students would object to sexually explicit language. There were parents to think of, too. No, he wasn't handing over the poem. Such smut wasn't going in the campus literary magazine, period. He'd stop the printing, if necessary. And while I was at it, I better think about cutting back on those four-letter words.

Tongue-tied with rage, I turned my back on him and walked out. Dozens of subversive thoughts jammed my head: I'd waylay him on a dark night, tar and feather him on the quad. . . . By the time I got back to the magazine office, my now-violated sanctuary, I was thinking along more constructive lines. I'd organize a campus-wide referendum on censorship, I'd instigate a letters-to-the-editor crusade, I'd plan a protest march. . . . But none of these ideas materialized either. Calmer, the very thought of battle sickened me. My editorial enthusiasm at the beginning of the school year had been undercut by the national grief, and now this challenge to my authority left me completely drained. The cause for literary freedom on a prurient drumlin, I mean who really cared? Tufts students didn't have to go far off campus to read shelves full of unexpurgated poetry and prose. Next door Cambridge with its bookshops and the multi-columned Widener Library, and Boston with its wondrously marbled-and-muraled public library—we were surrounded by temples to freedom of speech.

Quietly, I cancelled the imminent maelstrom. I guess it could be construed that I chickened out. But striking a revolutionary posture, being thoroughly nasty about it and risking the retaliatory wrath of the administration did not seem in keeping with the healing spring of 1964. In protest I upheld the gentlemanly model: a resignation submitted and accepted. I published the next issue of the magazine, and then I stepped down as editor. My concluding *Tuftonian* was larger and even more plebeian in content, a parting bouquet that took weeks of singleminded nurturing, and by the time it went to press, my assistants and I had cut so many classes we didn't feel like students anymore. I contributed plenty of my own material, beginning with a two-page editorial on censorship that paraphrased and discussed the missing poem to such a degree that it might as well have been included.

Stepping down as I did was unheard of. What rising senior would voluntarily give up so prestigious a position? The campus was rife with speculation; my enemies thought I had been bribed, my friends thought I had taken leave of my senses. What about my future? What about my résumé? As editor emeritus, I refused to contribute another word to the magazine, nor did my successor's publication interest me in the least. I was done with the literary scene, contented to turn pages of a more personal nature.

The detachment that characterized my senior year at Tufts was abetted by a blue motorcycle, a 50-cc Yamaha that ran on two-cycle fuel and got over a hundred miles to the gallon. It was the smallest, lightest street machine available—a glorified moped, really—that topped fifty on the flat with a tailwind. But handy it was, and convenient, and a charm to park as long as I took the precaution of chaining it to something that couldn't be carted off as easily as it could. By then I was dating a girl who went to school in western Massachusetts, so I needed an inexpensive form of transportation, but more to the point, I needed to redefine my image. No longer the gregarious campus fixture, I was aspiring to be an outsider. I wanted to create a place for myself on the fringe. If I wasn't exactly living dangerously, it seemed important to give the impression that I could have been.

With an engineer's cap for a crash helmet and thrift store riding leathers—a buttonless suede coat and vinyl boots—I must have cut an eccentric figure. When I wasn't on the road westward, a knuckle- and knee-freezing trip in cold weather, I made the nearer circuit—dropping in on Harvard Square, viewing the ocean at Marblehead, or cruising inland to Concord, where I'd circumambulate Walden Pond and contemplate the replica of the rude bridge that arched the flood. I zipped through the traffic on Storrow Drive and was in and out of downtown Boston in minutes. By late morning, when my last class was over, I could bowl a frame or two in Arlington at earlybird rates, then be in Fresh Pond for a blue plate special. Davis Square, Porter Square, Central Square—my haunts grew closer, merging into a series of short hops along a pick-and-choose afternoon. For the first time in my life, I wasn't dependent on someone else for transportation (nor on the racketing conveyances of the MTA). The youngest kid in class had finally come of age; a few pennies for gas, and I could be anywhere. As a student, my locus of inquiry widened. Greater Boston became my university.

Long before that final semester of riding days trailed off into an incomparable New England spring, my ability to concentrate on my studies at Tufts grew haphazard. Having been advised that everything was in order for me to receive my diploma—that is, if I got passing grades in my current coursework—I could afford to coast. Come hell or high water, I'd be finishing college, and that was the summa pro bona as far as my parents were concerned. I gave scant thought to what I'd be doing next. Nationally, the escalating commitment to Vietnam meant that the Selective Service would be breathing down my neck. Friends were going into the Peace Corps. Others were applying to graduate schools. ROTC was a missed opportunity, but perhaps I had been a pacifist all along.

And then it occurred to me that I had the perfect out: my much-neglected major in government. I could finesse military duty by joining the diplomatic corps. The half-baked dream of my freshman year could still come true. There were worse careers, and anyway, I'd only have to stay in the Foreign Service until the war in Southeast Asia wound down. Addis Ababa, Khartoum, Istanbul—the names of embassy postings lured me with their mystique. On a delegation clerk's salary I could save up for a new and larger street machine, tour exotic countrysides with a native love pressing close on the saddle behind me.

There was still time to take the FSEE (Foreign Service Entrance Exam). I made a hasty application just ahead of the deadline, and received a red-stamped admission ticket by return mail. It was too late to embark on a thorough review of government and history, not to mention math, languages, economics, and everything else, but I wasn't worried. This hurdle would be a low one, if standardized tests in the past (college boards and the like) were any indication. I figured I had enough general knowledge, and what I didn't know I could guess at. I had always prided myself on being an above-average guesser. Divination by multiple choice had long been a specialty of mine, a Zen thing like blindfolded archery, the pounce of the pencil point. Still, wary of being overconfident, I crammed. It wouldn't hurt to enlist at least a skeleton crew of facts and dates.

The slushy, late-winter morning arrived when I zipped over to a designated high school for the day-long, government-administered, combination aptitude and achievement test. Walking into the strange, Saturday classroom, bowlegged from the cold, I experienced sudden panic as I surveyed my competitive compatriots. These Foreign Service hopefuls looked like a brainy bunch. By contrast, my brain felt numb and my chilled facial muscles could barely move my mouth to form words. Fortuitously, I was assigned a chair by the window, so that I could thaw myself in the sun, if it ever came out.

Sealed test booklets and instructions were handed out, examination protocol was enunciated in harping decibels. When the sweep second hand of the clock crossed the vertical, we were commanded to begin. With a pre-chewed, government-issue electrographic pencil, I started blackening the slots, working rapidly, bending to the task vigorously enough, but as I turned page after page I felt my energy wane. I detested a test like this. There seemed to be a nefarious ambiguity to many of the multiple choice questions, which caused me to ponder the answers a fraction too long and thus penalize myself time-wise on the remaining ones. There were questions I simply could not bring my problem-solving skills to bear upon, and my answer-divining skills were depressingly out of kilter. Though I gamely guessed, too much of the stuff was way over my head. I had never heard of a certain hegemony. I had never studied such-and-such a treaty. Or was it dumb bad luck that I had ignored the droning professor when he covered these topics three years earlier in the lecture hall? Disconcerted, I crossed the throbbing threshold of a headache. This test was harder than I thought it would be. Instead of becoming a policy-implementing junior attaché, I'd be lucky to be assigned to the mailroom. Through page after page I struggled, guessing my brains out, leaping upon the rare question I knew the answer to, momentarily hung up on the abstruse. Under my right elbow, my answer sheet grew measly with pencilled jots, smeared every few centimeters with the rouge of erasements. I was encoding a wall of darkened windows, to be peered into by electronic sensors looking for a hidden order in the seeming randomness of my graphite marks. Evaluation by fenestration. In the windows, my flesh and blood hung in the balance. Shade up, shade up, shade down, shade up—my chance to become a Foreign Service officer depended on my shade pulling. What a stupid

137

thing I had done, majoring in government! What a stupid thing I was doing now, taking this ball-buster of a test. Working as quickly as I could, it felt like I was dead in the water.

I had at least six pages to go when I heard the stentorian, "Stop!" Three months later, the day after I graduated from Tufts, I received the bad news by registered mail: I had flunked the FSEE.

SEVENTEEN

THE TIMOTHY FIELDS ARE GREEN NOW, rivaling in verdancy the unrenovated fields across the fence. These newly planted acres have a whitish tinge like a dusting of sugar, a contrast to the mature sheen that characterizes the more established stands of orchard grass and fescue. A sheen or shine in nature signifies toughness—the armor of a carapace, the glaze of a pearl. The timothy presses tenderly underfoot, as if each bootfall will mash the life out of it. Even though the new grass grows densely, thanks to the lime and fertilizer so recently applied to the soil, I step gingerly, sparingly. I am the verderer, the keeper of the king's forest, the wanderer who will collect ticks on my pant legs as I survey the rolling, wind-waved domain and plan for its harvest.

I have been thinking a lot about the battlefield. Now that I am an old hand at reconstructing the Battle of Cross Keys, that singular whistle-stop in Stonewall Jackson's Shenandoah Valley campaign, I am subscribing to a higher dialectic. I would like to preserve this ground. The fact that our farm and its contiguous tracts share a footnote in American history is reason enough to be concerned for its future. But a hundred and thirty years have passed; the curve of population and progress is gathering momentum. Clearly, time is running out. Each successive year brings more houses, more poultry barns, more small businesses. Farmers, many of them already old, stave off retirement. Most will go right on working when they shouldn't; death will drop them in their traces—mid-furrow, as it were—amid family chaos and grief, and suddenly their farms will be put up for sale. More often than not, sons and daughters choose not to follow in a farming parent's footsteps. To break away from the drudgery and unpredictability and low profits and high property taxes is a farm inheritor's cherished dream. A savvy heir sees the land developers circling like vultures and welcomes their attention; if the cards are played right, a lifetime maintenance is in the offing. And so the story goes, the fragmentation of a family farm and its inevitable transformation into a subdivision, an industrial facility, a waste disposal site, or worse.

Thus far, the onus of preservation around Cross Keys has been a happy accident. One hundred thirty years is not that long in terms of property ownership: four generations, maybe three if there is longevity in the family. The virgin forests are gone, of course, and formerly cultivated fields are returning to scrub woods, or consigned to the limbo of pastureland. Those acres that continue to produce crops do so with the needling of fertilizer, which is usually applied annually, or even twice a year. The rules of twentieth-century agronomy read like a handbook of quick fixes, shortcuts, one-step solutions. Yet quite without conscious design, farming has promoted a stasis in the topography. The original property boundaries remain, and the oldest line fences, howsoever patched or prettified, convey a nineteenth-century irregularity. Farm lanes still wend along ancient right-of-ways. Modern farm buildings are in situ replacements of earlier sheds and barns. And though many are gone, enough old farmhouses still stand to convey the template (minus contemporary addenda) of the countryside circa 1860.

I know it won't last. Three years ago, a stoplight was installed at the crossroads. Three years hence, the backlit plastic franchise sign of a fast food outlet or a convenience store may be illuminating the cornfields. History buffs in the neighborhood swear, "Never!" but history buffs die. I say, "Never!" and I will die, too.

A clarion for the hobbling of progress often resounds in my brain. I've got to do something while I'm still here. I freely admit that my caring for the battlefield transcends the barbed-wire boundary of the forty acres I farm. Maybe I am sticking my nose into other people's business, but I don't think so. I consider myself a most unlikely candidate for proselytizing this or any cause, but someone's got to do something, or progress will see to it that our every option disappears and we'll be left with nothing but raised lettering on a highway plaque.

If only my neighbors' awareness of the local battle could be expanded a little! They need to be nudged vicariously into the nineteenth century, so they can see for themselves what it is they might want to preserve. Words I heard at the battlefield conference in Lexington, Kentucky — terms like "viewshed" and "easement" and "lifetime estate" — run through my mind. Without education, or at least some attempt at explanation, it is too big a burden to deal with history. Yet everybody knows that Civil War sites are abundant in this neck of the woods. Surely my neighbors will hear me out. They may even appreciate my well-meant pro-

posal to form a loosely knit, voluntary, and nonbinding property owners' alliance.

But before I make plans for the initial neighborhood get-together (to
be conducted in our living room on a Saturday afternoon, after the auctions and the livestock sales), I solicit an expert's help. In Lexington I
introduced myself to one of the guest speakers, the director of a
Washington D.C.-based, nonprofit organization dedicated to land conservation. I told her about the local battlefield, and she responded with
immediate interest. Now I have written her to ask if she'll be available
to chair our proposed meeting. She replies affirmatively. I am relieved
to let someone with such strong persuasive powers present my case.
Even in the role of a good and concerned neighbor, I would feel uncom-
fortable taking charge. I'm no good at extemporizing on my feet; I tend
to falter and turn red-faced. And anyway, I'm part of the problem. I built
a house and studios (not to mention a pond) on pristine battle acreage,
land that encompassed the very core of the infantry fight. At the time,
nobody could have stopped me. I was the biggest ignoramus of all.

A date for the meeting is set. It remains for me to notify my neighbors,
but I am loath to be too businesslike, too matter-of-fact. I'll be trying
to persuade farmers for the most part, country folk whose stewardship
of the land is a given—ancestrally so. Their mistrust of officialdom
knows no bounds, and by proxy, I am in that category just because I'm
an educated outsider—*a rocker of the boat*. When they open their doors
to greet me, a weathered skepticism permeates their stares. Most of these
neighbors know who I am ("Yer the feller who built way back in the
fields, right?"), and they've known me for seven years, but they still think
of me as a newcomer. In their vigilant eyes, I will remain so, and it's not
easy to launch a patter of bonhomie when I sense this intimidating mistrust. Briefly, I am tongue-tied as to the true reason for my visit. I start
by remarking on the weather or the rainfall, how I was just passing
through, commenting appreciatively about some aspect of house or
yard.

When I get around to the business at hand, my information comes
out in an undigestible lump, and I have to start over, one byte at a time,
one byte ahead of the other. "As you know, Ma'am (or Sir), your property is part of an area where a Civil War battle was fought. A lady from
Washington is coming (whoops, better backtrack here) a lady who
works with a nonprofit, *non*-governmental foundation that is interested
in the preservation of this land. . . ." Thus I work my spiel, trying to
sound as nonthreatening as possible, just folks talkin', and as I speak, I

search their faces for that spark of interest that would signal a little compassion for my cause. The spark, if it is there, escapes my attention. My words tumble out—too forced, too many. I wind up making a tepid plea for joining the bandwagon: "Well, I figured a bunch of us could meet over at my house and just listen to what this lady has to say. . . ." Crudely empathetic and even corny, I place myself at the mercy of my listener. I disguise my true feelings, pretending to be neutral, as if I were not the instigator of this, but just the bearer of the message, the go-between.

Yes, I know my guise is penetrable, but I'd feel naked without it. No neighbor has ever approached another neighbor on this topic. In rural Virginia, a property owner's rights are paramount and non-negotiable. He or she can do whatever the hell he or she wants to do; in Platonic terms, there is no greater good. A true native of Cross Keys wouldn't feel the necessity of bringing up the subject of preservation in the first place. The very thought of saving history smacks of socialism—government telling its citizens what do, instead of the other way around. In the cradle of States' Rights, the War of Northern Aggression rocks indefinitely. These notions are not stated *per se,* but they are implied in incremental nods and floor-cast glances. My exit cue is apparent. I repeat the date and time, expressing the hope that I'll see the person there, and I'm gone.

Weeks go by. As the day of the meeting approaches, I make my rounds again just to remind everybody. Better than a phone call, the personal touch, and my re-canvassing gets a warmer reception. Farmers, like elephants, don't forget. Of the dozen or so neighbors I have invited, at least nine or ten actually promise to show up. It is gratifying to know that my efforts haven't been totally in vain, but now I'm nervous. The director of the foundation telephones from Washington. I tell her everything's ready, but she better not set her expectations too high; she won't be lecturing the approving, informed audience she had in Kentucky. She laughs. She knows, she's done it before. Her disarming manner makes me realize I'm veering on a paranoid tangent. I've taken this thing as far as I can, and now I need to relax. She's the expert.

On the appointed day, her Lexus bumps down the lane and she emerges, gracious as I remembered her, poised and eager for business. She changes into sturdier footgear, and we set off on a tour of the battlefield.

By pickup truck and on foot, I show her the extent of the mile-wide line of battle—the horseshoe of hillocks onto which John C. Frémont's

Union artillery was drawn up by nine o'clock Sunday morning, June 8, 1862, and the corresponding bluff and flat-topped hill from which the Confederate forces under the command of Richard S. Ewell fired defensively. I try to describe the terrifying cannon duel that lasted until late afternoon. I trace for her the failed infantry advance on the Union left, an unanticipated bloodbath that resulted in a Confederate counter-charge and led to a forced Union withdrawal over more than a mile of ground. I describe additional Union infantry forays up the center and on the right that were headed for success until they were abruptly cancelled by Frémont, who was eager to conform his line of battle to the losses on his left, and call it a day.

I acquaint my visitor with the boundaries of the present-day farms that lie within this panorama, and I tell her what I know about their owners. Who's going broke, who's too sick to work, who's on the verge of retirement, who's getting ready to sell out. It's a sad litany, and as I rattle it off, I am struck by the timeliness of our endeavor. Most of the farms will be farmer-less before long. Land will be changing hands, and who knows what will happen then. Foreseen or not, the future is encroaching on the past; in twenty years or so, all that's left of the battlefield may be its name.

But it's time for the meeting, so my ruminations are cut short. Back at the house, I introduce my visitor to each neighbor; gratifyingly, almost all who said they'd come are here. When every chair is occupied in the rearranged living room, I rise to make a few opening remarks—words I have rehearsed all week in nightly bouts of insomnia. I begin by saying that the past hundred and thirty years have been kind to the battlefield, but the coming hundred and thirty years probably won't be, given the pressures and variables of growth in Rockingham County. We should empower ourselves to do something about it—we the people who actually live on the land, as opposed to the county supervisors, the planning and zoning commission, the blue ribbon panels, and so forth. My plea is standard anti-government rhetoric, designed to put everyone in a concordant mood. When I feel I've achieved this, I turn over the meeting to the expert from Washington.

She begins by explaining to my neighbors that she is their servant: she is employed by a nonprofit organization and thereby indirectly paid by their tax dollars. She is there to do their bidding, she says. It's an auspicious start, a ploy to win the approval of tax-oppressed farmers. She goes on to speak of community consensus, its benefits, and she strikes another sympathetic chord. Get everybody thinking alike, that's how to get

143

things done. But as soon as she gets down to the nuts and bolts of land preservation, I detect stirrings of disapproval in the living room, intimations of disunity.

She starts talking about easements. Property owners can have clauses written into deeds to restrict or even forbid future development. Owners can sell first refusals, so that preservationist organizations get first bids on historical properties as they come on the market. Encumbrances like these can be painless as well as financially rewarding; with a stroke of the pen, up to 80 percent of a property's value can be given to the owner in cold cash, with the title remaining in the owner's name. It's the perfect security for old age, but it does require that the property owner not sell or subdivide. The contract is also binding on the heirs.

Her listeners are shifting uncomfortably as she moves on to discuss voluntary restrictions and gifts. If further accumulation of money isn't necessary, why not give a gift to the community, to the nation? It's a sure way to be remembered after death. Citizens' bequests have been responsible for the salvation of numerous historical sites, she says, and she recounts a few well-known examples.

A portentous stillness descends on the assembly at this point, but she's unperturbed. Her cataract of information continues. There are things like lifetime estates to consider, whereby an owner sells his or her property but retains the right to live on it for the rest of his or her natural years. It's another painless option, and think of the taxes saved.

The stretched membrane of attentiveness ruptures. One gruff old farmer can't contain himself any longer. He's heard the options, he barks, and not a one of them's worth a hill of beans. This land is farmland, and the only way to keep farming it is to keep it in private ownership. A case in point is the Lee-Jackson property, a long-unfarmed ninety-six-acre tract (adjacent to our forty acres) that is owned by a non-profit foundation in Charlottesville. One look at the Lee-Jackson property (he says), and anyone can see how the good-intentioned, preservation-oriented folks from across the mountain have brought it to ruin. The tract is full of *filth*—his term for the cedars and thistles and honeysuckle that grow rampant—and it would take weeks of bulldozing to clean it up. This so-called preserved part of the battlefield is nothing but an eyesore to the community. To destroy perfectly good farmland this way is a crime.

The farmer goes on to relate how, some twenty years ago, he offered to buy the property from the Lee-Jackson Foundation and "bring it back" before the wild vegetation had gotten totally out of control. The

Foundation responded by putting so many encumbrances on the deed that it wouldn't have been ownership anymore, in his estimation. No, deed restrictions just don't work. These days, the incentive to farm can't be curtailed in any way. He strongly recommends that the Lee-Jackson property, if not sold outright, be leased rent-free to "a young feller with guts 'n' ambition" who will work hard to erase its advanced state of disuse.

At this point, another neighbor jumps in and says he would do it if he wasn't so dang busy holding down two outside jobs as well as running his farm. His solution would be to *pay* someone to come in and farm the Lee-Jackson property; barring that, the land should be sold to a developer. There's nothing wrong, he says, with a decently done cluster of townhouses that would increase the county's tax base and help relieve the tax burden on the poor farmer.

A woman from a nearby farm starts talking about how her husband's family has lived on their property for four generations. It is her children's birthright to inherit the place and dispose of it as they wish. She would not dream of entailing her family's land. She vehemently opposes any form of deed restriction. It smacks of communism, she says.

The owner of the farm adjacent to hers waxes discursively on the perils of big government. He, too, traces his lineage locally for generations. All his life, the town (Harrisonburg) has expanded in the direction of his farm, and now he is downright ticked off at the legal restrictions he must abide by. Why, just the other week he wanted to move an outbuilding—an equipment shed—from one side of the barnyard to another, but he couldn't do it without a *permit*. He likens the county supervisors to tinpot dictators, sitting behind big desks in shag-carpeted offices, bossing the people and taxing them to the hilt, then threatening them with fines or jail sentences if they disobey.

A farmer from another quarter, who is accompanied by a teenaged son wearing enormous basketball shoes, states that certain commodity prices—wheat and corn, for example—are the same today as they were in 1946, when he began farming. Meanwhile, inflation has shrunk the dollar by a factor of four. What's a farmer to do, he asks? He's farming his seventy acres with the first tractor he ever owned, a forty-year-old Oliver, and pulling many of his original implements, jury-rigged and cannibalized as they are. The price of fuel, lubricating oils, seed, and fertilizer has gone sky high. The last thing he wants is to be told what he can or cannot do by some silly deed restriction! That would be pure hell on a farmer.

The discussion becomes heated at this point. Voluntary preservation is seen as a fool's game; involuntary preservation is seen as a collusion between government and monied interest. The expert from Washington smiles an unflappable smile, but she is unable to get a word in edgewise. The genie is out of the bottle—the genie being the heartfelt defense of inalienable property rights, the bottle being the normal bashfulness of farming folk. Everyone's talking now, talking at once, agreeing vociferously that fewer restrictions, not more, are what's really needed.

As a sort of moderator, I attempt to steer the discussion in a more constructive direction. What does each person feel about the battlefield itself, I ask? Should it be preserved? And if so, can any person state specifically how he or she could contribute to its preservation?

A neighbor to the west says that one of her goals is to restore the antebellum house she lives in, which she looks upon as a lifelong project. But the Civil War is over-romanticized, she says. It's come, it's gone, and we all might as well forget about it. In her opinion, the saving of a battlefield is a narrow-interest preoccupation, given the nation's abundant social ills and injustices that need rectification.

The first farmer to speak reiterates that preservation as an end in itself is the wrong way to go about it. Preservation grows weeds. He's off on another diatribe about the Lee-Jackson land, but a retired Marine colonel, a board member of the Lee-Jackson Foundation whom I invited at the last minute, halts the charge. Tersely, the retired colonel observes that local people can't be counted on to value their unique heritage. He reminds the assembled guests that he hails from Fluvanna County, to the east of Charlottesville, where the natives don't give a damn about the past; outsiders have to run the historical society there, and it's a crying shame.

Another out-of-towner, the late-arriving director of a Fredericksburg-based preservationist organization, adds a graceful reminder. Civil War battlefields are fragile entities, almost like living things, he says. When they reach a certain level of degradation, they die, and they can never be brought back. They aren't appropriate for Disneyland. The war itself is too deeply embedded in America's consciousness for her citizens to ignore the fate of these battlefields. Our democratic political institutions owe their origins to rural acres where armed conflict occurred. If battlefields disappear, our society becomes rootless.

The farm wife interjects that she's fed up to here with do-good people who try to tell other people what to do with their property. The battlefield will always be there, she says, no matter what it looks like. You can't stop progress. She rises to excuse herself, haughtily pulling a large coat around her shoulders—a fleeting facsimile of Rodin's Balzac. One of her kids needs to be picked up from a riding lesson.

After she's gone, the level of discussion sinks even lower. All the bogeymen are re-trotted out, and a reactionary conservatism overpowers all constructive suggestions. Whether or not there's a battlefield in the vicinity is immaterial. Farmers just can't be expected to give up any more rights. The future recedes into an academic question; what matters is the here and now, and it stinks. The cataclysm of a Sunday morning in June 1862 is put on permanent hold.

Sensing this impasse, the expert from Washington adroitly cuts in to terminate the filibuster. Well, she says, this has been a most interesting and educational afternoon. She thanks everyone for coming. If anybody ever needs her help or her advice, they know where to reach her. End of meeting.

The guests are stretching their legs now and devouring the refreshments Becky and I laid out beforehand on the dining room table. There's a preternatural conviviality, it seems, an agreed-upon relief that the hard part is over. At least it's turning into a more positive experience, this afternoon of invective and bile. Half-sardonically, I continue to play the host as the gathering spills onto the porch and into the front yard. The Washingtonian is chatting with the Cross Keysians, and everyone's laughing and carrying on as though the acerbities never occurred. After a while, I am able to speak with her alone. Sotto voce, I apologize for the obdurateness of my neighbors. I sympathize with her for having gone through all this trouble to accomplish nothing.

"There's nothing to apologize for," she whispers conspiratorially. "Actually, I've accomplished rather much. Two farmers just told me privately that they'll be in touch. The son and daughter-in-law of that old codger to the east think that some day his home will make a fine museum. And the young man in those horrid sneakers, the one who'll inherit the seventy acres, came over and said I was 'right on.' "

EIGHTEEN

I HONESTLY DIDN'T KNOW WHAT TO DO. Plan A—the Foreign Service—was up in smoke. Plan B might as well have been to join the French Foreign Legion. That was the trouble: there was no Plan B. Tufts was done with me and I was done with Tufts. My friends had all left town, my room lease was up. I had raised what cash I could by selling my textbooks and furnishings. My possessions were pared down to a box of clothes, a sheaf of unfinished manuscript, a portfolio of watercolors—and my faithful steed, the blue Yamaha. I strapped what I had to the carrying rack and withdrew to New Jersey.

Arriving in Montclair, the first thing I noticed was a letter in the mailbox from the Selective Service. Greetings, it read. Having graduated from college, I was now reclassified 1-A, and would I please report for my physical in six weeks' time. Uncle Sam was requesting my presence. The call of the jungle.

It was June 1965, and to serve one's country without moral misgivings was no longer in vogue. The American military involvement in Southeast Asia was attracting increasing amounts of bad press, especially from the radical left. Folksingers deplored the war. College students were beginning to boycott ROTC programs. At rallies and lectures, the war's lethality was brought home with impressive—or horrific—statistics: body counts, bomb tonnages, troop and materièl increases. The pro-war flag-waving and anti-war flag-burning scared a civilian in my shoes; I'd be damned if I went and damned if I refused to go. I wasn't only afraid of getting killed (like any young person, I relished my right to be immortal), I couldn't bring myself to trust the judgment of the older generation. What greater proof of incompetency was there than the body bags that were filling? The times were a-changing, but the fuddy-duddies were still in charge—*this* was what I protested.

The physical wasn't scheduled until mid-July, so I was content to let matters slide. I was making my own decisions now; family life at home was a thing of the past. My parents were gone for the summer (my father was in Europe on a teaching sabbatical and my mother had joined him). My sister was living in Queens. My brother, fresh from his sophomore year at NYU, moved into the house with me, and together we eked out an aestival bachelorhood, freed of the constraints of parental supervision. Whatever misgivings my parents may have had about letting us live in the house by ourselves were entirely justified. We cranked up the volume of the living-room Magnavox so that it shook the crystal candlesticks on the doilies that were going pewter with dust. Classical LP's were banished to the back of the record bin to make way for our combined collection of rock 'n' roll. We stocked a goodly supply of liquor, importuning female companions to come over and help us drink it. In the mornings (if, indeed, it was morning when we woke up) we sat around and embellished the conquests of the night before, mapping out strategies for the weekend. We never mopped a floor or scrubbed a sink. Our breakfasts were "Instant," our dinners "TV." We did a load of laundry only when we absolutely had to; ditto for the countertop of dirty dishes.

Although the summer was shaping up to be an entertaining and relaxing one, I had industrious intentions. That first week home, I applied for a job as garbage collector—a vocation I thought might bolster the roman à clef I was trying to write. The previous summer I had been in France, in the foothills of the Jura, employed as an errand runner in a metal fabricators, and the summer before that, I had worked on the production line of an ice-cream factory in Paterson, New Jersey. I was eager to broaden the scope of my work experience, to transform minimum wage into something worth relating on the printed page.

By motorcycle, I zipped over to the town sanitation department headquarters where, like any other job applicant, I was handed a blank form. Under "Education," I proudly listed my credentials: Hillside School, Newark Academy, and now, my still-warm B.A. Unthinkingly, I blew it.

"What's this?" asked the surprised interviewer, who I guessed to be no less than a thirty-year veteran in the department. "You just graduated from college and you want to ride a shit wagon?"

I looked him straight in the eye. "Yessir, I do."

He scrutinized me like I was out of my mind. "That's the trouble with kids today," he began, and he up-ended a dumpsterful of philosophizing on my supposedly empty head as I stood there in front of his paper-littered steel desk. He said that kids like myself didn't value what parents struggled so hard to provide. When he was growing up (during the Depression years) it was different: to graduate from college was to receive a gift of opportunity, a promise of a better life. It took hard work to pay for an education, let alone make good grades. A degree of higher learning was nothing to take for granted. Neither he nor his nine siblings had gone to college, and not for lack of smarts. He went on in this vein, reminiscing about his own limited options and the many years he had spent in "shit gathering," as he called it—the injuries, the rats, the maggots. . . .

I wanted to interrupt and tell him that my aim was to *create* from the experience, to engage myself for the sake of art. I wanted to write from the point of view of a garbageman. I wanted to show him my draft reclassification letter, and confess to him that my life as a civilian was being cut short in a few weeks. But any rebuttal on my part would have appeared callow, given the extent and duration of his own sacrifice for his country. Men of his ilk were responsible for keeping the great wheels of consumerism turning. He spirited away the star-spangled refuse before it piled up on the streets and sidewalks.

Capping his peroration with a rejoinder about God and flag, he refused my application. He crushed it with one big hand and tossed it in the trash can. Garbage collectors didn't need college degrees, he said. In a word, I was overqualified.

Wiser now and playing dumb, I landed a job as a checkout clerk in a supermarket, an employment that lasted only three weeks because I couldn't handle the pressure of the checkout lane. Much as I tried to muster the blasé button-punching of a seasoned employee—and disburse the awesome drawerful of cash, and slam-dunk the groceries into brown bags—I couldn't keep up the pace. I was always double-checking, triple-checking. Customers' sotto voce urgings and six or seven loaded carts waiting in line couldn't speed me up. I didn't trust myself. This wasn't Monopoly money, these hard-earned dollars that were traded for junk food. I was too conscientious, and consequently I was a failure.

I figured I'd be better at nonremunerative, creative projects. I set up a painting easel in the sun porch, working mostly from still lifes—the rotting produce my brother and I purchased but neglected to eat. I began blocking out a frieze on the walls of the master bathroom. The History of Indoor Plumbing, I called it, a room surround of children bathing, women showering, men shaving, and solitary seated figures on commodes, *Thinker*-like, with skirts hiked and pants pulled down. My par-

ents wouldn't be totally freaked out, I reasoned, since they had sanc-
tioned murals in the basement, pietàs and such, when I had taken art
in junior high. (I was wrong; my mural-in-progress would be regarded
as a defacement—bathroom walls were for mirrors and towel racks,
nothing else.)

In addition, I continued writing, but I found it almost impossible to
get further than a brilliant opening sentence. The finely tuned crafting
of my editing days at Tufts had gone slack; I had grown wooden-headed
despite my steady stream of literary musings. Now it took two of me
to write: one person to sit still long enough to hew a line, and a second
person to rearrange the words into something readable. Being two people at once, woodcutter and carpenter, was excruciatingly difficult, and
it was made all the harder by an appalling dearth of subject matter. I was
jobless, approaching insolvency, bored, and boring. Quite literally, I believed that I had nothing to write about.

In college, being subject-less had led to vertiginous experiences with
writer's block. In such a state I had cast about desperately, but found
no act or phenomenon worthy of description. Only the need to achieve
a passing grade could goad me into action, often with piffling results. But
the summer in Montclair had no mandate other than its brevity. My
faculty for self-observation was whitened out. When I tried to conjure
up a train of words, I wound up with an empty track. I likened myself
to a car; my gas gauge of experience was on empty. How or when my
tank would fill was anybody's guess. In these borrowed quarters, on this
borrowed time, creativity in writing was nowhere to be found.

I tried getting out of the house. I'd ride into Newark just to sit on the
long wooden benches in the Newark Museum, notebook on lap, with
Joseph Stella's stupendous bridge beatifying a nearby wall. Waiting for
an inspirational *grand mal* was like waiting for Godot. I'd bike up to
Eagle Rock, the hogback outcropping to the west, where the panorama
of greater New York twinkled and millions of people went about their
minuscule agendas while airplanes lazily circled Newark Airport with
their landing gear down. Nope, no inspiration there, either. The distant
line of Manhattan skyscrapers was just another picket fence. I'd close my
notebook with a dull slap, hitch my pen to my pocket, and head back
down the hill.

The day arrived when I was summoned for my Selective Service physical, which, in spite of my lack of a balanced diet and my penchant for
staying up till the wee hours, I passed with flying colors. The draft board
informed me that another greeting, this one from an Army Induction

Center, would be winging my way within a month. But soon after being declared so physically fit, I came down with mononucleosis – the kissing disease, as some call it, although it was more likely a reaction to this sudden acceleration of fate than oscular promiscuity. I got sicker and sicker with a listless, running fever that kept me in bed in the stuffy, unkempt house during the crest of a mosquito-slapping Jersey heat wave. My brother summoned the family physician (the first and last house call I had ever known the busy medico to make), who told me, in effect, to keep lying there. In a daze, I watched the world go by – the world I could not describe in words, the world I could no longer paint, the world that was about to rubber-stamp me into cannon fodder.

I could not go gently. I could not stay in bed for the rest of the summer, waiting to get better as I prepared for the worst. Feverish and with a raging sore throat, I accepted an invitation to spend a weekend on Block Island – off the Rhode Island coast – at the summer home of the family of a girl I was dating. Ironically, both her parents were medical doctors, but I breathed not a word of my discomfort. I rode to New England in the back seat of their Cadillac, croaking a feigned joviality, sweating even in the air conditioning. For once, I kept my hands to myself, and the girl kept asking, "Are you all right? Are you *sure* you're all right?" I lied that I was. It was strange to be passing through the haunts of my childhood – Kingston, Narragansett, Galilee – as a sickly, introspective passenger. It seemed that my formative years were closed off from me forever. The places I recognized through the tinted glass were paste-ups from the pages of someone else's scrapbook, not substantive, not real. I had not done a good job of preserving them (for the moment, I was doing a poor job of preserving myself). I had not made them come alive in painting or prose. Speeding past, I had no deeper sensibility than Herr and Frau Doktor in the front seat, eyes glued to the highway, ears attuned to the stereophonic lieder of Easy Listening.

On Block Island, I felt even worse. The sun and wind beat down on my aching limbs, and the surf, usually a blessed balm, imposed a Mixmaster-like chaos upon my fragile equilibrium. The sea cure was killing me. On the front porch, wrapped in a blanket, I shuttered myself from the elements. The good doctors came and went, sun-visored and clad in beach togs, a *Wall Street Journal* or *Business Week* tucked under an arm. Breezing past me, they'd inquire if anything was wrong, but I assured them I was fine. I didn't dare tell them the truth. To be ill (and possibly contagious) would be interpreted as an ingratitude. The last thing I wanted to do was spoil their vacation, and anyway, they probably thought that my being immobilized was keeping their daughter out of harm's way. Unable to lure me beach-side after that first afternoon, she was contenting herself with solitary, day-long tanning sessions.

Somehow, I got through the weekend and was returned to New Jersey, whereupon I dropped back into bed. Another few weeks of convalescence, and I began to feel better. My induction notice from the army arrived by special delivery. Time was running out. Mornings of promise were disappearing one by one; besides, I was broke. My brother had headed back across the Hudson River for his junior year, my sister (a rare visitor) was still ensconced in Queens, on the verge of graduate school, and my parents were still junketing the Continent, marveling in frequent postcards at the culture and cuisine of the Old World. I was the rat on the sinking ship.

The girl I was dating had gone off to college in Pittsburgh, and now she was writing perfumed missives telling me how much she missed me. Pittsburgh was a great place, she said, full of neat people, lots of nifty things to do, but she was *lonely*—underscored thrice—and her rotund script trailed off in shorthand for love and kisses. Feeling my old self by now, her written sighs were all the cue I needed. I had become a one-day-at-a-timer. I decided to sell my motorcycle and go to Pittsburgh on the proceeds.

On such short notice, my best chance of getting rid of the Yamaha was at the dealership where I had purchased it new, the Harley-Davidson shop two townships east of Montclair. I packed my toothbrush and a change of underwear, and carefully locking the door to the house of sickness and stagnation, I strapped my pitiful package on the chrome rack. Then I retracted the kickstand and trod the diminutive foot crank for the last time—my Zipmobile, my beloved sewing machine, my maze-unbender and friend. With my feet on the familiar footpegs, I steered a valedictory course through the traffic on Bloomfield Avenue.

The Harley salesman recognized me right away and seemed to understand the urgency of the transaction. Giving me a hundred and fifty dollars cash, he invited me to come back when I was out of the army and ready to move up to a Hog. Okay, I'd remember that. And when my wallet was truly fat, I'd invest in a wallet chain, too.

Sitting in the half-empty intercity bus as it jounced toward Port Authority Terminal, I reflected on my loss of dependable, two-wheeled transportation. Yes, I'd be happy to go whole hog, live high on the hog, and eventually go to hog heaven, if I wasn't so hog-tied. I was about to suffer the greatest loss of them all — the loss of my freedom. Once I was drafted, I'd become a number, a stamping on a dogtag, and if I was unlucky, that old ringing bell, *freedom*, would toll again and again for me. He died in the defense of freedom. Clang. He was a freedom fighter who made the ultimate sacrifice. Clang, clang. In freedom's name, we honor the deceased. Clang. Freedom was a morbid word. Fuck freedom.

But in the meanwhile, the sands were still running. I was deposited on the fumious upper deck of the bus terminal, and carefree it felt to alight in Manhattan — to grasp the soothing handrail of the escalator, to walk the terrazzo floor to everywhere and nowhere. I mingled with travelers and bystanders, drug-dealers and the homeless. For the first time in my life I, too, was homeless. Anonymously, I strolled the familiar reaches of the terminal, peering into the shops, the snack bars, the newsstands. Watchful eyes may have imagined some pernicious agenda behind my lackadaisical gait, but if ever there was an innocent, it was I. Rounding an unpopulated corner outside the waiting room, I was suddenly confronted by a desperate-looking individual in tattered clothing. Loudly, he demanded my money. Holy shit, a mugger! Momentarily, I was paralyzed. I didn't know what to do or say. How did he know I was carrying a wad of cash? Damn, there goes Pittsburgh!

The derelict laughed in my frightened face and walked away. I was just another mark, and I should have seen him coming, but he rattled me, he really did. I wolfed down a hot dog and soda, then procured my one-way ticket without delay. My nerves were stretched rubber bands. My overt wariness and guarded gait were too revealing. I decided that terminal-roaming with no safety net other than that which was stuffed deeply into my breast pocket was best postponed until departure time. I retired to the busiest quadrant of the waiting room and breathed the body odor of a somnolent, overweight matron who looked about as dangerous as my grandmother.

Of the overnight bus ride across the Alleghenies, I remember little except the rumbling indigo turnpike grades and yellow-lit tunnels. I slept as much as I could with my arms protectively folded across my chest. On arrival, the girl was there to meet me (from the waiting room in New York, I had called her person-to-person, speaking with her at length and squandering no small portion of my remaining capital). We breakfasted next door to the bus station, and, as always, it was my treat.

I found a room in a boardinghouse in Shadyside, near to her campus, paying the landlady two weeks in advance — the two weeks that remained of my civilian existence. What was left of my nest egg would be spent on food, with my last twenty dollars in reserve for bus fare to the army induction center at Fort Bragg, New Jersey.

In my apprehensive condition, I became unduly cognizant of flowers. Pittsburgh seemed to be a city of flowers that September. Flowers delineated sidewalks, burdened windowboxes, buttressed foundations – and in my rented room, the floral leitmotif blossomed in overlapping abundance. There were nosegays of forget-me-nots on the wallpaper, plastic daffodils in vases, lilies and lilacs creased along the curtains, a daisy chain on the throw rug, chenille peonies tufting the bedspread. A pinkish-raspberry tinge suffused the room – a light so suggestively warm that the dust motes could have been minute embers in suspension. By evening it felt like we were bedding down in a gaudy hothouse. On an end table, a rose-patterned lampshade glowed a parchment coral, and the girl's gardenia scent accompanied the antique bedstead's minuet of squeaks and scrapes.

Anticipating weeks if not months of privation, I wanted to preserve this girl, preserve her in my mind. The best way to do that, I thought, was to paint her nude portrait, an idea to which she readily acquiesced. Deciding it was possible to subsist on fewer meals per day, I bought a pre-stretched canvas, a couple of brushes, some tubes of oil paint and some turpentine, and we set to work – she seated by the window and I standing at an armoire that served as my palette table, the canvas propped against one edge of its mirror. An hour here, an hour there between her classes, and our sessions slowly began to bear fruit. Inspiration was the shy handmaiden of desperation. But I needed more paint, more time, and it disturbed me that my subject was not endowed with a professional model's imperturbability. I bought a tube of yellow oxide, then burnt sienna, then naphthol red, then cadmium orange, then a larger tube of flake white, and then I realized I was at an impasse. The figure on my canvas looked stiff, amateurish. I couldn't for the life of me make the right corrections. My patience was wearing thin, and the girl would not shed her clothes so easily now. I was taking up too much of her time, she said. Her classes were being neglected. She felt guilty, she felt stupid. She got goosebumps, she was so cold. Clearly, Herr and Frau Doktor retained a powerful grip from afar. Our Matisse-mimicking had become a passionless procedure in a rose-colored room, and I was accused of making impossible demands.

The portrait was put on indefinite hold. On some days, she was too busy to see me at all. I was ready to fold the tent, but much to my consternation, I realized I had spent my busfare to Fort Bragg on the extra oil colors. It behooved me to walk downtown to the armed forces recruiting center to explain my predicament. It was a walk of several miles, not unpleasant. Even the staring flowers seemed to understand that I was too poor to afford public transportation, and too proud to borrow fifty cents from the girl. Every footstep was a lower increment in the countdown. Blast-off was a day, maybe two, away.

As I walked in the door of the recruiting center, a navy noncom was quick to capitalize on the confused—and perhaps hungry—look on my face. Over desktop doughnuts and coffee, he told me that I could enlist in the Naval Reserve, and thus bypass the army induction altogether. I'd have to serve a two-year hitch, beginning with four months or so of boot camp, but chances were that I'd pull East Coast duty, not West Coast and 'Nam. Upon discharge, there'd be two more years in the reserves—one weekend a month and refresher training for two weeks every summer. My other option, since I was a college graduate, was to go to Officer Candidate School and become an officer in the Naval Reserve, but that was a three-year hitch, with two additional years of weekend and summer duty. Whichever way, it was a better deal than being a grunt in the jungle.

Think it over, he said, but I saw my situation with perfervid clarity: I needed to traverse the quicksand of active duty by the swiftest, safest route. I enlisted that morning in the Naval Reserve, then I walked back to Shadyside to tell the girl what I'd done. The following day I was booked on a one-way flight to Chicago, where I'd catch a train to Waukegan, Illinois, home of the Great Lakes Naval Training Center. The girl took the news with a tear in her eye. That night we ate peanut-butter sandwiches in the copiously blooming bower and made promises both of us knew were meaningless and bound to be broken, tormenting each other with an almost-new, one-night sensuality. I never finished her portrait.

NINETEEN

W HEN I'M NOT MAKING HAY, fixing farm machinery, or looking after forty labor-demanding acres, I am producing art; but I guess this sentence would be more truthful the other way around: when I'm not practicing as an artist, I'm busy doing everything else. I am thankful that I spend a good deal of time painting. I work in a large, concrete-floored studio off to one side of our house. Becky has a slightly smaller studio off to the other side of the house — hers doesn't hold a grand piano.

My career as an abstract painter is seen by many people, including a few close relatives, as a delusion. They see a man approaching fifty, mired in a quest that has accumulated no payoff much less gotten off the ground. They see stacks of unsold paintings leaning against the studio walls (and if they care to look, they'll find similar stacks in the basement and barn). Disinterestedly, they can flip through several decades' worth of sundry periods and styles — from my earliest lingerie ad imitations to my latest battlefield depictions — and they can shake their heads, tsk-tsking why in heaven's name didn't a person of my education and background go into a more lucrative field?

Some of these people are worldly to the nth degree about everything except abstract art. They've read the right books, they've seen the right movies, they talk the right talk, but when it comes to nonobjective painting, they're babes in the woods. They haven't the faintest idea what they're looking at, what they're *supposed* to be looking at. They turn to me expectantly, as if it's up to me to provide the key with a verbal explanation.

Whether these people come to my studio with sincere, or merely polite curiosity, they are almost always let down, for try as I might, my words fail to lift their veil of incomprehension. It's no great secret that the majority of art lovers prefer to look at a recognizable image. It doesn't matter if that image is rendered with first-rate ingenuity or third-rate maladroitness, or if it is tattered or fractured or redistributed to the extreme, or if its hues have passed through the prism of make believe. If something is identifiable, even vaguely so, it serves as a tether to reality by which the human eye can chain itself before taking on the vaguer precepts of the dream world. My paintings don't always include that nicety.

Every good artist populates his or her works with dreams. It is central to artistry of any sort that an alternative to reality be offered the viewer. Why certain viewers shrink from that alternative when it goes too far out on a limb, when it detaches itself completely from visually observed phenomena, I'll never know. Dreams "go out on a limb," don't they? A good artist's dreams delve into the unknown, and thus, the viewer undergoes the requisite reaction, referred to by some as the Aesthetic Experience.

Most viewers are good burghers like me, which means that when their *composure sorta slips* — that is to say, when they're provoked by art — they're also entertained. I paint abstractly and nonobjectively because the best kind of visual expression I am capable of does not necessarily ground itself in what I see. The painting is the thing itself. My art is a conceptual and expressive discipline. For me to achieve an appealing visual dexterity, that is, a painting that works, I need to tap the visionary landscape that is in my head. No one can see it except me, and I'm not so sure I see it as much as I feel it. At a relatively young age I realized that, for my purposes, the beaux art approach to visual expression would not alone suffice, although I learned it as well as anybody. The art lessons I took as a child in Rhode Island went easily enough (at age eight, I was featured in the *Providence Evening Journal* for a painting I had done of a giraffe), but even then I preferred to depict the stylized subject that was in my mind rather than the bare-bones subject before my eyes.

The world sighted is a gift from God — a blind person will agree — and I do not diminish its value. To see a thing and quantify its contours, its dimensions, its color, its texture is to unwrap the gift slowly, savoring the image. Learning to draw and paint can be an incredibly satisfying personal achievement, as it certainly was for me. Art hobbyists are inhabitants of high places, presidents and prime ministers among the more preeminent practitioners. Art as recreation must rate a close third to sex and drinking. Making art can calm disturbed emotions, too; thus it becomes a therapy for the mentally disadvantaged. Put a paintbrush in the hand of someone who's out of control, and his or her fractiousness will be assuaged, maybe even transformed into something cheery and violent for all the world to appreciate. Nouveau Van Gogh.

But the vocational pursuit of art – I feel compelled to repeat this sentence-starter because it peals the truth – the *vocational* pursuit of art is not an easy or relaxing business. Firstly, an artist competes with his or her nonartistic self – in my case, the hayfarmer and family man – and secondly, an artist competes with his or her peers. Competition among visual artists is intense; it has always been so, since the depicting of hunters' wish lists and derring-do on cave walls. The Flemish and Dutch and Italian ateliers were full of wanna-be's. There were a bevy more French Impressionists than Monet, Renoir, Bonnard, Pisarro, et al. Nowadays, members of the art profession number in the tens of thousands – worldwide, in the *hundreds* of thousands – and at the pinnacle (where the action is) are a handful of practitioners whose name recognition and singularity of style shine forth with a never-dimming light. That these blue-chippers have been in the public eye long enough to become self-caricatures is unimportant. They're at the top, edging out everybody else, and they're staying put until they die. There's no place else for them to go, given the thralldom of fame. Their work gets bigger, bolder, more bombastic. They clone, they replicate. Museums clamor for one of each.

For every good artist, there are at least a hundred bad artists, and for every famous artist, there are at least a thousand good artists. I know exactly where I fit in. I am neither expectant of nor apprehensive of fame. In the contemporary pantheon, my bronze bust will probably never gain admittance, if the past thirty years are any indication, although I can't be sure. I've been to enough antique stores and estate auctions to know that almost everything accumulates value over the years. Clothing, bedding, jugs, mason jars, broken tools – every humble thing rises to prominence as surely as an air bubble rises to the water's surface. Who knows, there might even be a demand someday for the used razor blades dropped through slots in medicine cabinets as early icons of the twentieth century's throwaway culture. Or, for that matter, our descendants may be enshrining landfills.

But abstract, nonobjective paintings, cobwebbed and crazed with time – it's hard to predict their ultimate desirability. The end of painting was announced decades ago. Between themselves, Frank Stella and Helen Frankenthaler (and maybe five or six others) wrapped up the last noteworthy experiments. My work fits squarely in the middle of the Post-Significant addenda, between the last gasp of expressionism and the death-rattle of postmodernism. In a future world of laserlight and computer projections (sometimes referred to as "virtual reality"), a painting other than a pedigreed, highly varnished old masterwork may not survive. Rembrandt *si*, Svenson *non*. Painting with a paintbrush on canvas has already become the Model T of visual expression. The genre has simply gone out of style. Microprocessors, digital displays, and evolving software whip up doodles to really boggle a viewer's mind. There's a good chance that my paintings will be bulldozed with the barn, or razed with the house and studios when Battlefield Estates comes to pass (if preservation nose-dives after I am gone).

I was an unquestioning believer in Progress when I set out to paint professionally. I fully expected to contribute meaningfully to society's grand scheme—and to reap just compensation. Now I am somewhat skeptical, but still cheerful. Even though I can't recommend an artistic career as a growth industry, it doesn't mean I'm giving up. I am as Western as Western can be, I just keep plugging away. I don't believe in Progress anymore, but who does? Progress, American-style, has been the very thing that has let me down, and I am not alone. I am but one of a great number of creative individuals who struggle against the tide. One glance at my body of unsold work—canvas after canvas with few or no recognizable referents—and a maverick commonality emerges. I'm no assembly line, I'm no rubber stamp. I am proud of myself, I think. Or maybe I am disgusted. Whichever way, it takes a blend of optimism and innocence to stay the course when there's almost always no reward at the end. Nonplussed, I continue to stand at the easel day after day.

But the truth is, I've given up on plenty of occasions. Zephyrs of fashion in the art world have shifted my style all too frequently. What conscientious artist is not a weathervane? The chances for commercial success have pointed me toward any number of dead ends. I've listened to umpteen gallery directors expound on trends that either petered out or became oversaturated with practitioners. I've swung in the breezes of bad advice. My abandonment of lost causes, once I realized they were lost, is a record that burns in my brain on a bad day; time after time, I've followed the promising paths to nowhere.

Indeed, I have taken great pains to preserve my career as an artist, and to preserve my output. But when an artist's oeuvre becomes a storage problem, something has gone wrong. Paintings are meant to hang on walls, not lean against them. My work should be disseminated to the far reaches of civilization by now, not just sequestered around the farm.

I made the choice years ago to live in rural Virginia instead of New York City, where like-minded aficionados of abstraction can at least congregate to pat each other on the back. I travel there every few months to make the rounds, armed with a portable painting or two, and I invariably give the impression that I don't belong. Being the outsider, the bushwacker, the boondocker is a role somebody has to play, I suppose. When I'm street-walking with a cumbersome portfolio case, I'm incapable of divulging the other facets of my life. The farmer and family man is on hold while I undertake the task of presenting my wares to the cognoscenti. To jaded eyes that winnow through such a surfeit of art, my paintings cannot possibly stand out, and I, their creator, must stand out even less—a graybeard interloper with the acclimatized vestige of a Southern accent.

Between visits northward, I endeavor to promote my work as best I can. I keep a steady stream of photographic slides circulating in the mail. I regularly send off letters of inquiry, flimsy door-busters to which I only rarely receive a reply. The trouble is, stamped, self-addressed envelopes are not chainsaws. By proxy and in the flesh, I don't make a spectacle of myself; maybe that's why I usually don't succeed.

In Virginia, when the average person meets me on the street or at a party and learns that I am an abstract artist, he or she is quick to rein in the friendliness. In the sanctum sanctorums of SoHo, I meet a similarly chilly reception. It's a lose-lose situation: on the one hand, I'm rejected for being too weird, and on the other hand I'm rejected for being too ordinary. Self-preservation at this point becomes problematical. Either place, I'm there at the wrong time with the wrong credentials. Is it any wonder that I retreat to the privacy of my studio in the far corner of the hayfield where, drawing and painting, I can lick my wounds?

In pursuit of a viable career as a painter, I do my best to dodge the ignominies, the biggest of which is being flat broke. Over the years, my livelihood has been supplemented by a series of short-term jobs, and during times of grave insolvency, I have been reduced, as aforementioned, to selling possessions. (One lean winter I even sold the heating stove out of my studio.) But when I came to the battlefield and plunged into hay farming, I gradually gave up most of my sundry employments. For the first time in my life, I knew I would be able to make an income that, though supplemental to my wife's, was enough to get by on. After devoting a full year to building our house and studios, I could hardly wait to put down the hammer and saw and pick up the paintbrush. The urge to get back to painting was almost like hunger or thirst—the longer I staved it off, the weaker I felt.

Deep down, during the long months of construction, I wondered if

I ever *could* paint again. For an artist, a year of not producing art can be a dangerous sojourn. If painting was truly dead, as the critics said, how was I to resurrect it? My career in art bore no resemblance to a phoenix; repressed for so long and now cancelled for the duration, I wasn't sure if it would rise from the ashes. For the first time ever, I came close to losing my nerve. All the diversions—the transferral of a sense of place, the overseeing of forty acres, the housebuilding—had crowded out my heretofore engrossing sense of self. In the past, I had been careful to conserve a core of artistry during an extended leave from the studio; I sketched, looked at art books, went to galleries, consulted with other artists—but this time, I was just too busy. I accomplished nothing but strenuous physical labor, and at the end of the workday I was thoroughly bushed. What spare energy I mustered was directed toward learning about the Civil War, its scarring of the very ground I toiled upon. My interest began as pure escapism, but turned into something more: a commitment to preserve the battlefield by uncovering its story.

I found my way back into painting by riding the coattails, as it were, of the Battle of Cross Keys. Although it took me nearly five years to get around to painting specific battle themes—abstractly, of course—I must have been gestating the necessary thoughts, spin-offs of fact and commotion from the hundred-and-twenty-some-year-old fight. I began identifying with the Civil War battle because I, too, was embattled. It was a strange joinery: a twentieth-century misfit and a nineteenth-century military event.

The story of the battle, as it came to light for me, only deepened my identification. I found out, for example, that immigrant soldiers—raw recruits from the streets of New York City, who barely spoke a word of English—fought for the Union side and suffered horrendous casualties. Wasn't I an immigrant too, an artist with a "New York" sensibility come to live in the farmland of Virginia's Shenandoah Valley? The Confederate general most responsible for the success of the battle was Isaac R. Trimble, an energetic old man who bucked the authority of his younger superiors. No longer young, I was still fighting the battle for artistic recognition, Trimble-esque in my role and hopeful for an eventual vindication.

Today, my sense of identification is more detached. I see the battle period in my art as a distinct one that flared invigoratingly—and led to an oeuvre that I was fortunate enough to exhibit—before it cooled. Although I remain very much entranced by what I imagine the local eruption of the Civil War was like, I've removed myself aesthetically only

164

because I dwelled on it so intensely for so long. The paraphernalia of warfare is still strewn about my studio—crudded paintbrushes, paint-encrusted palette knives, mixing sticks fat with color, de-stretched canvases, used staples, leftover lattice ends. There's also a low stock of paint. The splatters on the floor, multicolored though they be, are the very drops of soldier's blood. I was that soldier.

Now I stand in front of my easel and consider more peaceful scenarios. Whether I want it to be or not, my anonymity as an artist is probably preserved. I'm still on square one, still ready to prove to the world that I have what it takes. I guess it all boils down to this: I like to paint, I need to paint, and I'm not bad at it.

TWENTY

Dᴜʀɪɴɢ ᴍʏ ᴇɪɢʜᴛᴇᴇɴ ᴡᴇᴇᴋs in boot camp, I did my best to preserve the core of my being—no small job considering the cumulative effects of fatigue, exercise, and indoctrination that living in a unit of similarly scalped, homesick strangers entailed. Disciplined by marching, conditioned by repetitive drills, stuffed with the skills of seamanship, I feared that my individuality might disappear altogether. We were a company of a hundred young men, one of a score of companies in progression through the conveyor belt of basic training. I was just another seaman recruit, a male American nobody in flapping flannels, a chief petty officer's object of scorn, a nincompoop on the way to becoming a Navy Man.

I could be ordered to do pushups for imagined infractions, or be deprived of sleep by standing guard duty all night in the snoring dormitory. I marched on a tarmac called the Grinder until my legs lost sensation and the bellowed command, "Company, *halt!*" seemed like a reprieve from the Almighty. I was a deck-swabber, a latrine-cleaner, a shoe-shiner who was conditioned to shriek, "Yes, *Sir!*" and "No, *Sir!*" in the presence of imbeciles of higher rank. I learned the mechanics of a smart salute. I was both wearer and washer of government-issue clothing. Naked, I stood in a line of recruits while the "pecker-checker" peered at our private parts, inspecting for sexually transmitted diseases (to the rear, with our buttocks splayed, he looked for hemorrhoids). In another line, I received immunizations right and left from high-pressure injection guns that drove nails of serum into my upper arms.

The only college graduate in my company, I found myself forgetting that I had ever gone to college. For the first time, oddly, I was the oldest person in my peer group (many of the recruits were right out of high school). Inner city boys, farm boys, small town boys—our demographic mirrored the nation, and most of us had this in common: we had chosen an honorable alternative to army duty in Vietnam. Because of my education, I was designated company clerk, the caller of the roll, but aside from that, I did exactly what everyone else did. We looked the same, thought the same, dreamed the same. Under the continuous strain of being yelled at, our esprit de corps developed quickly, the civilian in each of us subsumed a little more each day until, mentally as well as physically, we recoiled with perfect obedience.

"Hurry up and wait," was the unofficial boot camp motto. In a typical twenty-four hours we were persuaded, plied, pushed, pontificated to, and pilloried, beginning with reveille at four-thirty in the morning. We were marched to the mess hall for breakfast as dawn broke through the fall-enflamed trees that lined the avenues between barracks. Mornings were spent learning seamanship and performing calisthenics. By lunchtime, it didn't matter what was dished onto our stainless steel trays; we stoked the calories any way we could. Then we stood inspections, went to more classes, practiced drills, participated in small-arms training, and marched in formation until chow call late in the afternoon. Evenings in the company barracks afforded an hour or two for relaxation and letter writing, but only after the washing and folding of uniforms, the polishing of shoes, and the general "squaring away" of all gear. By lights out at 2100 hours, sleep struck like a sledge hammer.

Today, nearly thirty years later, navy boot camp may be an ameliorated experience made comfortable by advances in consumer gadgetry and the politically correct, nonsexist protection of the child within, but back in the 1960s it was strictly no-frills. For the first few weeks there were no televisions or radios, no books or magazines, no incoming mail, and no contact with the outside world except a three-minute, once-a-week phone call. On arrival, a recruit was supposed to strip himself of his civilian possessions, which were immediately boxed and shipped to his home address. (A day later, his every hidden keepsake was ferreted out by force and taken away for good—thus I forfeited a cherished Boy Scout knife that had belonged to my grandfather.) The regulation haircut came next, then the issuance of a seabag of regulation clothing. The deprivation and isolation made the real world seem distantly suspended in time. Job vacancies filled, kinfolk moved away, girlfriends stopped waiting, and we weren't the wiser.

But as the days and weeks wore on, it was easy to see that boot camp was, indeed, an efficient instrument by which to prepare teenaged civilians for active military service. We were *shaping up*. On Thanksgiving Day, with a month of basic training to go, every person in the company was given a twelve-hour liberty pass to ride the train into Chicago; it was the least the navy could do to preserve that second-best of American holidays. The foretaste of freedom generated ear-to-ear grins, hyperbole of hopefulness. To be off base for half a day would be a chance to explore heaven itself. But on the speeding, double-decker coach, some practical joker kept yelling, "*Attention on deck!*" causing every recruit to jerk to his feet in marionette-like compliance to the frequently heard command. We chuckled over the incidents all the way to Chicago, but inwardly I was distraught. As one of the automatic standees, I kept glancing wildly about to see who the asshole of an officer was who barked me out of my comfortable seat. My individuality had been sufficiently negated to succumb to the pratfall over and over.

As more weeks went by, a leaner, less-introspective person walked in my penitentiary-made brogues. I was getting used to the boot camp routine, not actively disliking it, though I still counted the days (who didn't?) till graduation. I grew increasingly curious about the ship I'd pull duty on, and where she'd be home-ported. I fervently prayed not to be sent to the West Coast. Our company commander, an Irishman and chief petty officer with a coat forearm ablaze in red sateen slashes that symbolized consecutive four-year enlistments, was no longer such a tough bastard. Now that the company was shaping up to his satisfaction, his bluster metamorphosed into something paternal and benevolent. His leadership actually inspired us. After hours, he'd regale us with crazy stories of bar-hopping and whoring at exotic ports of call, himself in the role of the swaggerer who knew when and how to extricate his drinking buddies from indelicate situations. He made sea duty seem like fun—the yo-ho-ho-and-a-bottle-of-rum stuff of chanteys. He personified a tradition that went back to *Old Ironsides* and square rigging, and his example made us dress all the smarter and march all the harder.

But with two weeks to go to graduation, I came down with a bad cold that developed into pneumonia. Seasonal viruses were rampant in our close quarters; everyone sniffled and coughed and expectorated sideways when marching in formation. I tried to hang on as long as I could, but a worsening congestion got the better of me. Two fellow recruits had to practically carry me to sickbay. For a week I lay delirious on a cot in a crowded ward, breathing with difficulty, unable to swallow the pills that were proffered with cups of Kool-aid. It was spooky to hear taps played over the loudspeaker when a recruit died (this happened at least twice during my stay). Like my bout with mononucleosis a few months earlier, my illness made me contemplate the abandonment of self-preservation. My hopes for graduating with my company were dashed. I missed my buddies. I missed my parents, my brother and sister, my on-again-off-again girlfriend. I missed the company commander, who personally arrived at sickbay with the bad news that I would have to be "set back." In his gruff way, he was affirming the good news that I would live, which I had begun to doubt.

And he was right: with absolute rest, my body began to heal. Wheezing lungfuls of phlegm were gradually broken up. At length ambulatory, I shuffled around the ward in a government-issue bathrobe with a paper cup in hand—my portable spittoon.

I finished boot camp in a later company, buddyless and ten pounds lighter, a pale add-on from sickbay who was excused by written order from standing night watches. Right before I was granted my graduation leave, I learned that I had been billeted on an oiler, the USS *Chikaskia* (AO-54), a World War II-era tanker that was home-ported in Norfolk, Virginia. At least one prayer had been answered.

Two weeks later, the night bus to Norfolk deposited me pierside to a submarine tender. The *Big Chik*, as she was called, was moored two ships outboard. With seabag slung over my shoulder and orders in hand, I climbed the accomodation ladder to the tender, crossing its broad deck then walking the gangplank to an auxiliary supply ship known as a reefer, crossing it amidships, too, before navigating a narrower gangplank to the ship that would be my home for the remainder of my two-year enlistment. This stroll across the water, saluting the quarterdeck watches and the stern flags thrice, stepping on the shadows of my peacoated self under the glare of floodlight booms, inhaling shipboard aromas for the first time and hearing the ubiquitous whine of ventilation systems—this disjointed, shoulder-weary stroll past abutments of battleship gray in a calm, midnight mooring was my real introduction to the navy.

I was escorted to a third-tier bunk belowdecks, assigned an empty locker (and told to put a padlock on it as soon as possible to discourage thievery), then given a hushed tour of crew quarters. Since it was a liberty night in port, many sailors were ashore, though by dribs and drabs they were returning aboard, a few of them careening drunk, foulmouthed and belligerent with white hats askew. My fresh uniform with its newly sewn on seaman third-class stripes made me fair game.

"Well, looky here!" A sailor several sheets to the wind poked a forefinger into my neckerchief. "Green as grass. Kiss my ass. Welcome to the rust-bucket navy!"

The tour resumed, I was shown the head—the shipboard term for latrine—with its dimpled freshwater-economizing sinks and seawater commodes. I was shown the mess deck, which gleamed dully of aluminum and buffed asphalt tile. I saw the galley, the ship's store, the brig that doubled as a paint locker. The ladder to "officers' country" was pointed out to me, and I was admonished not to climb it unless specifically authorized.

That the *Chikaskia* was a superannuated vessel in the auxiliary fleet was plain to see. Her superstructures fore and aft sat squarishly upright, while her bow flared in a snub-nosed, old-fashioned way. Compared to a modern oiler, she was short in length and narrow of beam, with a comically outsized funnel above her aft quarters. The Little Oiler That Could. Flanking the funnel were two three-inch gun pods, canvas-shrouded relics of the battle action she had seen back in the 1940s when she steamed the Pacific. Above her well deck—the lowest area between superstructures where her tank wells were lined up like gray stumps— was a cluttered forest of refueling rigs: booms, winches, hoses trussed up by cable. The mission of a fleet oiler was to replenish other navy vessels at sea, an operation that required steady helmsmanship and an all-hands effort. Aside from her predominant cargo of bunker oil, the *Chikaskia* also carried AvGas and JP-5 (aviation gasoline, jet fuel), volatile hydrocarbons that could blow the ship sky high if their tanks were accidentally ignited.

As such, oiler duty posed inherent risks, although I quickly learned, as a member of the two-hundred-man crew, that the average sailor gave little thought to incipient incineration. If the AvGas tank blew, it blew. An oiler sailor's fatalism underscored his pride. The *Chik* was no ship of the line, no gun or missile platform, but at best a wallowing target, the necessary logistical support for a smart formation at sea—a milch cow. Her sailors loved her and hated her in equal measure. Pride, as I felt it here, was a strong identification with the imperfect world. "This man's navy," as the expression went, was not the spit-and-polish, squared-away fighting force that patrolled the oceans as America's teeth-bared ambassadors. This was the auxiliary fleet, the work-horse navy, that kept the carriers and cruisers on station, and it didn't matter if a crew member's dungarees were stained with a little black oil, or if his white hat was smudged.

Like the elderly lady that she was, the USS *Chikaskia* had reached an age of continual breakdowns. If it wasn't her boilers or her generators or her evaporators, it was her steam lines that were rupturing, or her pumps weren't pumping, or her steering was on the blink. She had been commissioned before I was born, mothballed through the 1950s, then recommissioned at the start of the Vietnam-era buildup. Her hull plates were buckled by heavy seas and scaled with corrosion, and her decks and bulkheads had been roughened by face-lifts from chip-hammers and air-chisels during yard overhauls. Re-paintings preserved the deeper indentations. Both abovedecks and below, the retro-fitting of improved equipment left the ship looking as though she had survived a series of reincarnations. She bristled with new radar masts and communications antennae. She had new CO_2 lines snaking along her bulkheads for smothering fuel fires. The cumulative effect of the overhauls made the ship appear top-heavy, laden with extras to bring her up-to-date. Where old equipment had been there were welding scars and bolts that bolted nothing.

Most of the time she sat in port like a permanently moored fuel barge, riding high because her tanks were empty, or nearly so, seemingly the last ship in the fleet to be given sailing orders. On the occasions when she left her mooring, her first port of call was always Craney Island, a fuel depot on the Portsmouth side of Hampton Roads, where her tanks were filled. Waiting for the hull to settle to the Plimsoll line was a relaxing week-long procedure. Craney Island was a bird sanctuary out in the middle of nowhere, a vast wetland enhanced by the volumetric scenery of the tank farm, a rail-gazer's no-smoking zone. When her freeboard was reduced to about eight feet, the old oiler was tug-nudged into the shipping channel, and if all systems were responding to the engine order telegraph, she set out to sea, usually accompanied by other auxiliary ships.

On station somewhere in the Atlantic we'd steam in circles for days, replenishing as needed, at times practicing the retrieval of a dummy Apollo capsule (we never witnessed a real splash-down), at times engaging in general quarters drills, man-overboard drills, or any other drills the captain could dream up as we breasted the swells at quarter speed, awaiting further commands from fleet headquarters.

Every once in a while, the captain received permission to make a high speed run — a sort of showing-off of battle readiness — that, for the *Big Chik*, was a twelve-knot rolling gait that warmed the crew quarters from the extra heat generated by the engine room. Beauteous black smoke billowed from her prominent funnel. Bunks, food trays, lockers — everything shuddered and shook, and abovedecks it was a novelty to watch the accelerated slipping-by of the water and the rarely glimpsed vee of foam from the bow wave. Unfortunately, the strain of a high-speed run would almost always hasten another breakdown of the propulsion system, which would necessitate our limping back to port.

Periodically we'd be caught in the midst of an Atlantic storm, whereupon the *Chik* wallowed precipitously, pitching bow and stern in wind-whipped crashes of spray, her well deck submerged in the roiling sea, the whole ship quivering with vibration whenever her screws breached the water. In a moderate-to-heavy swell, 100 percent of her crew was seasick. Abunk or clutching the railing, a sailor's faith in the old tub wavered. In calmer waters, during one voyage or another, every hand had been assigned to a work detail at the bottom of one of her empty tanks, work that involved mopping up the crud and sinter that had settled out from the bunker oil (and could potentially foul an off-loading pump). "Mucking" the tanks was a rite of initiation, an oiler sailor's equatorial crossing. When eyes adjusted to the dark, everyone saw for himself how bashed and rusted the ship's hull plates were on the inside. There in the odoriferous depths, with daylight streaming down the skeletal series of ladders from the open well-cover fifty feet above, a sailor saw the unpainted essence of what kept him afloat, and it was not reassuring.

Because of my education—that standing-out-like-a-sore-thumb credential—I was assigned to the ship's supply office, where I served as a storekeeper. My most pressing duty was to keep track of requisitions for repair parts via a paper trail that went from file box to file box on punched cards, frequently analyzed or averaged by adding machine. Since I could type, I was also the office typist, the person who transformed the supply officer's syntax-less verbiage into official correspondence. As a seaman third class, my superiors volunteered me for "work parties" as they arose—carrying supplies aboard, inventorying parts, maintaining storage spaces, and so forth. I was also assigned a lookout station on the signal bridge, the highest point on the forward superstructure, whenever the ship got under way. I stood there as a backup pair of eyes to the regular crew on the navigation bridge, one deck below. With a telephone headset and a pair of binoculars, I called out the buoys and channel markers and water traffic ahead, but I don't think anybody ever paid any attention to me.

All my shipboard duties were hour-consuming and rote, but some were more enjoyable than others. I liked standing the quarterdeck watch whenever the ship was in port. In four-hour increments, it was a watch stood in twos—an officer or petty officer and a seaman—a tradition as old as the navy itself. A naval vessel's quarterdeck was its welcome mat, a space roped off with fancy knotting and projectile casings, a showplace for ship's plaques and service awards. On watch, I received the salute of anyone who came aboard, and I piped announcements (including reveille and taps) through the PA system. I also kept an hourly log of the ship's mooring status.

An uneventful four-hour watch for me and my designated superior was a rare chance for one-on-one conversation, a temporary suspension of rank and seniority. It allowed for an intellectual give-and-take that was almost always prohibited by the exigencies of normal shipboard communication (enlisted personnel were forbidden to fraternize with officers, and vice versa). The white guard belt I wore imbued me with a feeling of being in charge; the heavily holstered Colt .45 with its loaded ammunition clip was a solemn reminder of preparedness. As a watchstander, I could snack anytime, and drink all the coffee or Coke I needed to stay awake. And whenever I pulled the 0400 to 0800 rotation, I had first dibs on the fresh doughnuts that arrived at sunrise.

Barring watch duty, my regular work hours were spent in the supply office at the stern of the ship. There I made two early friends—Short Hall and Tall Hall. Short Hall was a six-year enlistee who had recently resolved not to "re-up," a lifer who changed his mind. Tall Hall was a two-year reservist like me. Short Hall was an Alabama redneck who harbored a visceral dislike of Yankees, especially college-educated ones, until I won him over with attention and respect. Tall Hall was a neurasthenic newlywed who availed himself in every off-duty hour to be with his wife and baby-on-the-way in their tawdry garden apartment in Norfolk. Short Hall showed me the ropes, Tall Hall taught me not to worry about them. Short Hall knew how to "skate" and take advantage of the "bennies"—in other words, not work too hard and live it up a little at the navy's expense. Tall Hall was a math whiz with a sense of humor; when the requisitions piled up and the OPTAR (Operational Target, the navy acronym for a ship's budget) figures failed to add up, he tilted back on his government-issue swivel chair and snickered delightedly. Short Hall and I became boon companions on liberty nights on the "strip" outside the gates of NOB (Naval Operating Base). At sea, Tall Hall and I were unbeatable whist partners, thanks to our original bidding conventions.

I have always tried to preserve the cast of characters in the supply office because when I think back on the individual personalities, I lose sight of the privation and regimentation of my two years before the mast, and I am happier for it.

There was Vandecamp, our anorexic chief petty officer who felt it his first duty to peddle a cleaning solvent called Swipe. According to Vandecamp, Swipe was the world's foremost scientifically formulated antidote to grime, and the Lord had put him on a navy oiler to prove his point. The spray bottle grail was available in quart, half-gallon, and gallon sizes, with a special discount on orders by the case. Demonstration scrubbings (decks, desktops, bulkheads, etc.) were accompanied by incessant sloganeering ("Just one little wipe with Swipe"), and as Swipe's emissary to the fleet, Vandecamp was personally available to take orders day or night. He conned the brass to let him try it down in the bottom of the tanks. He donated a case to the scullery. He recommended it for cars, pets, rugs, windows, bathtubs, and bloodstains. He envisioned greater Norfolk, nay, Western Civilization itself, spanking clean and sparklingly disinfected thanks to this Miracle Product. Though he requisitioned quite a bit of the elixer for shipboard use, it never caught on because it had a rather strong smell and tended to irritate the skin.

Next in the pecking order was O'Grady-Reade, petty officer first class, a thirty-year man, efficient and proper, but also a compulsive gambler and a beseeching borrower of money. At the desk beside him was Mallory, a busted seaman and college dropout, convivial to a fault, a person congenitally unable to suppress his broad South Carolinian smile. Since Mallory was a short-timer, soon to be discharged, he disencumbered himself of all responsibility, employing his talents in the pursuit of various off-beat projects. For instance, he went to great lengths to prove that a match-flame turned blue in the vicinity of flatulence. Mallory could be counted on to mess up the books, but he was such a likeable fellow that nobody, not even O'Grady-Reade, who was his biggest debtor, gave him much flak.

Then there was Honeycutt, who repeatedly went AWOL, and Garcia, a strapping teenager from Minnesota, who came aboard after I did, thus easing my bottom-of-the-pecking-order status. And Richardson, the manic former advertising guy from Detroit, keyholder in the Playboy Club, curator of a pinup museum within the confines of his locker. His sidekick was Warburg—seasick even in port, but with a world-class repertoire of off-color jokes. These enlisted personnel, myself included, served under two officers, Lieutenant (Junior Grade) Meyerbeer—the one who couldn't write a business letter—and Ensign Kosciusko, a shy fellow with a harelip's croon few could understand. Between the six or eight of us on duty at any given time, the supply work got done, and if it didn't, it got so buried under the mountain of paperwork that it rolled over into the next fiscal year and vanished in invisible ink.

There was the right way, the wrong way, and the navy way, as I learned. Accounting procedures were no exception. On board ship, it was customary to spend leftover funds (from the quarterly budget) by ordering brand new replacements for items in use—repair parts or other pieces of equipment—to ensure that the budget never got cut back. To clear the books, the replaced items had to be virtually tossed down the memory hole. They could not be reconditioned or refurbished, or auctioned off, or passed on to the needy, or given away. They had to disappear, and quickly. This procedure was called *surveying*. When the ship was out at sea (or sometimes even in port) the replaced equipment was simply thrown overboard.

I still have pangs of guilt from being ordered to heave a perfectly good typewriter over the rail. It was an Underwood Office Standard, an industrial-strength typewriter (the same indestructible gunmetal model I have only recently abandoned for a word processor), and undoubtedly it had sat on a desk in the supply office since the christening of the ship. During working hours, I typed official correspondence on it, and after hours, I typed love letters, letters home, and redrafts of my ever-lingering roman à clef. I was its ribbon changer, its most frequent user. I begged Lieutenant Meyerbeer to let me preserve the old thing, to let me spirit it down the gangplank in the dark of night, if necessary—but no, navy regs forbade that sort of foolishness, he said. To cure my attachment, I was selected to provide the coup de grace. Under Meyerbeer's baleful eye, I lifted the machine from the steel desk and carried it to the fantail. As the noble Underwood flew from my hands and struck the churning wake, I said a benediction and pictured it descending the pressure-pure deep, where in the space of a minute, perhaps, it would leave its final imprint, its own four-footed frame, in the primeval mud.

The new typewriter I uncrated and placed on the desk was an electric import with a swooping, beige-painted pot-metal exterior, and its solenoidal eagerness kept tripping up my fingers.

TWENTY-ONE

ART AND FARMING ARE TWO unlikely occupations, and I see now that I have bridged them with another striving that has been a sort of silent partner all these years—my writing. And I cannot discuss my writing without mentioning in the same breath my reading. Words have been kind to me; they nourished me when I had a child's hunger for worldliness, they comforted me when I had trouble making headway in my creative forays, and they continue to sustain me as the building blocks of real and vicarious experience. At times, I think I am the luckiest person alive: I am never at a loss for words.

Because it has been so within my grasp, writing has been my best means of self-preservation. It started out, at age three or four, as a kind of visual longing, a yearning to set down amorphous impressions that were filling me with a scribal imperative. I seem to have wanted to write even before I knew what writing was. The limitations of my undeveloped state required me to put my contemplations down as crude marks that had significance only to me. To my parents, little Peter was drawing, and so I was—yet without saying so, I was really trying to produce words.

Long before I went to kindergarten, the spines of the shelved books in the living room intrigued me; I remember lying on the floor staring at them for what must have been hours. The shelves' unevenness appealed to me—colors, contours, thicknesses, heights. Jacketed or bare, each spine extended a personal invitation that I knew I was at a loss to act upon. I could only marvel at the way the volumes had been emplaced, upright or aslant or piled flat so that I occasionally caught a gleam of gold leaf. The dust on the books gave them a venerability unlike the magazines, which were also piled nearby, dog-eared and drooping like flaccid paperbound counterfeits. I had observed that magazines were utilized on an ongoing basis, and as such, could be left carelessly in the singular on the arm of a chair or at the corner of a table. Books were thicker, sturdier, and their ranks were rarely, if ever, broken. I had an idea what reading was, even though I didn't know how to read. Reading was the interpretation of someone else's writing. Being the true repositories for reading and writing, books were one-time experiences, but precious and perhaps holy ones, and so they remained shelf-bound to serve as mementos, souvenirs of hallowed thought.

As I lay there contemplating the books as objects, grownup objects, I noticed how different they were from the brightly colored children's versions that were thrust, in all their tiresomeness, under my nose when I was told to be quiet. The volumes I was given to "read" seemed far too slender to be worthy of serious attention. Yes, I loved flipping their pages and following the exploits of the puppy or the locomotive, and the tugboat had such sad eyes that I almost cried to think of its upcoming predicament, but *these were not real books!* They didn't have the weight, the sheared flat brick of paper, and within them was not that multi-paged, multi-lined wrinkledness boxed within ivory-white margins, each page with a belly-button numeral at top or bottom. Books were a mystery I was determined to unravel, but in the meantime, visual appreciation sufficed.

I remember choosing one book from the shelf for my very own possession: a small but chubby azure volume (as soon as I was old enough to read, I learned it was a pocket dictionary of musical terms) that had flexible covers and an attached gilt ribbon for marking one's place in its papery treasury of hieroglyphs. Without question, it was the cutest book on the bookshelf, a talismanic handful, and my adoption of it had a very definite purpose. This book would teach me to write. I recall "studying" it with great care, feeling sure that once I had mastered it, I could produce something similar on my own, and thus add my handiwork to the side-by-side sacrosanctity that weighed down the shelving.

Not long afterward I was creating miniature tomes from used mimeo paper, cut as carefully as could be with a dull pair of bandage scissors, and bound with an unsatisfactory accretion of staples from the stapler on my father's desk in a series of palm-bruising punches that only partially penetrated the accumulated thickness. By the time I was done, I had rendered my few pages dreadfully skewed and their binding hazardous to the fingertips. My volumes were created first, then they were written on. Somewhere in the bottom of a box in the barn, I've preserved one or two of them (and I've got others, a generation newer, that were created by my own children).

The innocent lettering capsizes and about-faces, skittering off the diminutive pages—on the verso of which are meaningless chunks of purple print—and there is frequent resort to pictographs to get the point across. A child's first attempt at writing is the most beautiful calligraphy in the world. A pre-schooler's self-made books are an unforced marriage of the verbal and the visual, and a celebration of *objectness*, too. Professionally aping these dawning inspirations, adults whose métier is the literature of early childhood strive to recapture the innocence. But slickness will always creep into an ex-child's imagination, while real children are by and large immune to slickness—at least they used to be. I certainly was. Much as I enjoyed the children's books at the Kingston library (and perused just about every one at least a dozen times), I found that my own product kept me more entertained, even after I was finished making it.

As I grew up, my efforts at writing acquired the onus of contributing to my livelihood, and this diluted their entertainment value for me. It began to look silly to staple my works together and pronounce them books. To write meant to write for others, and thus I entered the world of query letters and self-addressed stamped envelopes. It was not a world I could claim much success in, but being in it at all meant that I had made the transition from child writer to literary adult.

Only decades later, when I discovered the Civil War on forty acres of hayfield in the Shenandoah Valley, did my long-lost fascination with writing return. The Battle of Cross Keys was underfoot and in the air I breathed. Like my parents' bookshelf, it captivated my attention. I realized that I had been aware of the Civil War since childhood; in effect, I had borne witness to the war's aftermath for most of my life, living in its twentieth-century shadow, inheriting the collective wisdom of its heroes and heroines. Still, I was looking at the war without truly fathoming its particulars. The war had become a compilation of signs and symbols, fodder for my ignorance, but now, on my battlefield farm, it was also becoming something I could not tear myself away from.

My ancestry seems to have been only slightly affected by the events of the 1860s. On my mother's side there was a great uncle who had been a colonel in the quartermaster corps of the Union Army, while my father's side had yet to disembark at Ellis Island. As a very young child, my mother watched the old Yankee soldiers (they were in their seventies and eighties by then) marching on Veterans Day from Grant's Tomb along Riverside Drive in New York City to the Soldiers and Sailors Monument. Of the Southern point of view, I was handed down a profound, close-lipped ignorance.

Yet the war had touched my early childhood in several indelible ways. First, there was a book, a children's illustrated history of the Civil War—published in the 1880s, an heirloom from my mother's side of the family—that was kept in a paper bag on an upper shelf because its binding was falling apart. When I was allowed to remove the book to shorten a rainy afternoon, I found its didacticism enormously entertaining. In large print and monosyllabically divided words (accompanied by hand-tinted color plates that made reality seem drab by comparison) the four-year upheaval was simplistically spelled out. Battle after magnificent battle leaped off the brittle pages. Infantries swarmed, fortifications bristled, fife-and-drum corps paraded. Brass-buttoned blue- or gray-frock-coated commanders on rearing steeds personified valor amid finely cross-hatched billows of cannon smoke. Among the most moving scenes were the surrenders—the orderly line-ups, the doffed chapeaus, the proffered swords.

Second, there were artifacts that had been handed down: a leaded brass belt buckle (US, of course), some shoulder insignias, an assortment of uniform buttons. Not much, but enough to reconstruct a soldier if I let my imagination connect the dots. And last there was music—melodies I'd come upon quite by accident in the heavy, holed envelopes of my parents' numerous albums of 78s: Marian Anderson singing "The Battle Hymn"; a Dixieland "Dixie"; a deeply dramatized "When Johnny Comes Marching Home"; "Lorena," as haunting a tune as I'd ever heard or ever will hear. Certain lyrics perplexed me with their sadness: "In the prison cell I sit thinking, Mother dear, of you," for example. I was steeped in a brew of Civil War emotions without even knowing it.

Throughout elementary school, the war was a rote mantle behind the noble figure of Abraham Lincoln. All the nineteenth-century complexities had been distilled to twentieth-century truisms: Lincoln brought the South to its knees, Lincoln freed the slaves, Lincoln spoke in homespun homilies, Lincoln was assassinated by John Wilkes Booth. From penny to five-dollar bill, from enthroned marble to cracked-glass negative, his gaunt and bearded visage was a reminder of the salutary wholeness that had come after four years of civil strife. The president appeared larger than the war. I thought Lincoln must have been about eight feet tall, made even taller by his stovepipe hat. Even Lincoln's counterpart in Richmond, Jefferson Davis (who slightly resembled him), enhanced the illusion by being a dark double, a penumbra who caused the Emancipator to shine all the brighter.

Later, in civics class in junior high, the war took up a major part of the scholastic year. Along the vernier of nation-shaping conflicts – the French and Indian War, the Revolutionary War, the War of 1812 – the Civil War was the first extensive detour that warranted class projects and special homework assignments. I remember constructing a plaster-of-paris model of Fort Sumter. I painted a poster of the *Monitor* and the *Merrimac* slugging it out in Hampton Roads. I made a slouch cap from my father's shirt cardboards. And in more academic moments, I memorized the Gettysburg Address and crammed for quizzes in which the statecraft of secessionism taxed my short-term memory.

Much later, at the far end of my secondary schooling when the war's centennial rolled around, I was exposed anew to the facts and artifacts that were trotted out for the occasion. The national preoccupation with self-examination, as it related to the Civil War, was in high renaissance. Restorations, refurbishment, re-enactments – the backward view unfolded as if it were one gigantic history lesson, a reminder to the American people that the nation had passed through its self-inflicted trauma with flying colors and was doing fine. The centennial was like a clean bill of health for the next hundred, if not the next thousand years. For a new generation, *Gone with the Wind* wound through the sprockets in projection booths across the land. Book-wise, the centennial spawned a bevy of instant hits: best-selling blockbuster treatises, newly discovered soldiers' journals, acres of period fiction, and the ubiquitous impressarios for the coffee table.

I was in the throes of a post-adolescent agnosticism by then, and I remember being leery of the hoopla. The nation had fought two (and a half) wars on the outside in the present century; its populace was looking back with nostalgia to the previous century's "inside" war. But the self-back-patting did not square with the bigotry and inequality I saw all around me. It seemed to me that the fabric made whole by the Gettysburg Address was continually rent by razor-sharp hatreds.

Wasn't the Civil War actually being preserved in this centennial celebration? Not for me. The present had outstripped the past. As a product of my times, I saw the centennial as a green light for wholesale forgetfulness about what had actually happened. It's almost as though the *science* of the American Civil War was begun around then, and because of its complexity and undue attention to recaptured lacunae, it excluded me from developing more than a passing interest. I tried to read the books, but I never got very far into them. I went to look at the monuments, but they were meaningless marble pedestals. Battlefield, schmattlefield – what about the Nazi concentration camps? What about

Hiroshima? What about the daily promise of Armageddon that the locked horns of capitalism and communism were threatening to deliver on—the nullification that would be sprung from below-ground silos and undersea stalkers?

So, to develop the analogy, I was looking at the Civil War the same way that, as a child, I lay on the floor looking at the books on my parents' bookshelf, entertained but uncomprehending because I didn't know how to read. I realized I had looked at the Civil War in this uncomprehending way all my life. The monuments and books and movies weren't really doing the job. The war in its entirety was too awesome, its issues too labyrinthine, and by that same token the war was dead, as dead as its soldiers beneath the flag-fluttering fleets of marble in the national cemeteries. No matter what I tried, I couldn't bring any of it back. My comprehension wasn't to gain purchase for another twenty years, not until I was digging a basement excavation in ground where thousands had fought and hundreds had perished.

Between the painting and the farming at Cross Keys, my writing began to assert itself as I gained my sense of place and history. Old-fashioned curiosity was my starting point. There was a story to be told about this ground—I felt it in my bones. Unearthing the details of the Battle of Cross Keys was a project I didn't think I could fail at. I knew I could become a good sleuth if I wanted to; years of developing largely self-taught skills left me with the confidence to learn one more. I began scribbling down my research on index cards, then on legal pads, then in a bound journal. I saw the direction in which I was headed, and I did not waver. I went headlong into the process of my own re-education. To write knowledgeably about one battle in the Civil War meant that I had to dip seriously into that bookshelf to end all bookshelves—the 90,000-plus published works that cover the trauma and tragedy of the 1860s from almost every conceivable angle.

Time was my biggest expense. No grant was funding me, no promissory carrot from a publisher was dangled before me. I began the task with no guarantee that the fruits of my labor would ever reward me, much less sustain me in a financial way. As I struggled with my research, I began to see how interwoven my own life was with my subject matter. Initially, the realization threw me into a dither; the added complications meant the abandonment of a linear narrative that could function in a single time frame. Although I aspired to preserve the battlefield's story, I wanted to write about it in its present context as well as its past. I had my own story to tell too.

182

After months of organizational attempts and false starts, a glimmer of marketability appeared on the horizon. The local newspaper announced several openings for weekly columnists. Suddenly, I had a terrific column idea: I would write about the forty acres and I would call it "Battlefield Beat." I conceived it as a commentary on nature and the seasons, on weekends with my children, on my work in both artistic and agricultural fields, and as I was acquainting myself with the facts pertaining to the battle, I would write about them as well. For years I had tried to land employment along these lines—writing descriptively on the installment plan, and getting paid for the results.

Well, the one or two sample columns I submitted were rejected with a polite note. I should try again in six months. I did. My efforts were rejected anew. Like the slide sheets of paintings, like the manuscripts of so many earlier writing projects that were slammed back in the mailbox in return envelopes postmarked from everywhere but home—these brave little columns came back to me unused. Instead, the newspaper readers were treated to locally bred expository writing on Christian homemaking, on puns by the tons, on car care. My audience remained a figment of my imagination. I was ready to abandon the battlefield idea and look for another subject—some other topic to parlay into the journalistic equivalent of the hula hoop. I prided myself on my ability to bounce back. For years, I had been telling people that Rejection was my middle name.

But the battlefield wouldn't let go of me, nor would the battle that materialized as I gained knowedge of and insight into its particulars. All I can say is that a divine wind—for lack of a better term—kept blowing me along. I continued to write as I crossed and recrossed the bridge between painting and farming, and the outcome, after two additional years of literary toil, has been what could be characterized as a Happy Beginning, a net promise that makes the effort seem worth it. I have an audience now, one that responds to my words in a way I could only have dreamed of during the first four-and-four-fifths decades of my life. My words have survived the transition from marks to misspellings to manageable prose, and finally they appear between two covers, potentially to collect dust but also to collect readers—or, for that matter, onlookers. I have won an inch of space on the bookshelf.

TWENTY-TWO

Having benefited from sixteen weeks in drydock in Baltimore, and following that, a two-week shakedown cruise to GITMO (Guantánamo Bay), the good ship *Chikaskia* was ready to set sail for the Mediterranean in July 1967 on a six-month deployment with the Sixth Fleet. I would have enjoyed the change of scenery – the blueness, the balminess, and the ports of call of a Med-cruise – but there was a problem: I was a short-timer with only three more months of active duty. My overriding priority was to return to civilian life on schedule.

But my problem went deeper. I had a mortal fear of being a passenger on a breeches buoy. If my enlistment expired while the oiler was at sea, that was how I'd get off her. There was no helipad on the *Chik*. During seagoing replenishment when the breeches buoy was strung by cable between ships, life-jacketed transferees, seabags hugged to their chests, were pulled dangling one at a time over the water. The deck-apes (the boatswain's mates who shot the line gun, rigged the highline, and manned the pulley) sometimes took a perverse pleasure in dunking the chair, which, from the vantage point of its occupant, must have been nothing short of terrifying. Any time that fuel hoses were stretched between ships, a breakaway situation was possible. Too often I had heard the wail of the emergency klaxon as the *Chikaskia* and its succorer got out of synch. Either veering apart or about to collide, the two tethered vessels wavered, causing moments of anxious suspense, and I had seen the corridor between them become a writhing tangle of hastily cut cables and oil-spewing six-inch hoses. No, I would not ride the chair.

One night in the supply office, less than a week before the *Chik* was to depart for the Mediterranean, I typed a fake document to cancel this eventuality. It purported to be a letter from the dean of New York University's graduate school of business, congratulating me on my immediate acceptance for the fall semester. (Earlier, I had procured a sheet of NYU letterhead from my father's desk.) The next morning at mail call, I made a big to-do about my "acceptance" letter, waving it under Lieutenant Meyerbeer's nose, uttering great groans of regret about how much I wanted to go on the cruise, how much I'd miss my buddies, and so forth. It was the classic Uncle Remus shtick, and it worked. Meyerbeer wrote me an "effective immediately" transfer, which was initialed without comment by successive higher ups. I gained new respect for the convincingness of an electric typewriter. In all probability, Meyerbeer had been smart like a fox, seizing on the opportunity to get rid of me, for as a short-timer I had grown increasingly lackadaisical—an attitude he may have construed as deleterious to supply office morale.

At any rate, I vacated locker and bunk, swapped farewells with my shipmates, and walked down the accomodation ladder at Craney Island for the last time. On a gray bench beside a gray trash barrel, I waited for the shuttle van to NOB and took a last, lingering look at *Big Chik*. She lay moored to the pierside maze of pipes and valves, her stern markedly lower than her bow as her cargo tanks were onloaded one by one. It would be a long cruise; topped off, she'd cross the Atlantic low in the water. There was talk that she might be decommissioned afterward. Welling with sentimentality, I realized I would always preserve the least part of her. I wished her and her crew well. For all her breakdowns and mishaps and lengthy periods of inactivity, and for all her seasickness-inducing meanders upon the high seas, I had grown to love her. For nearly seventeen months she had been my home. She floated on faith, on her bellyful of bunker oil, and it seemed strange that her scent of unburned liquid hydrocarbon would waft henceforth only in my memory.

I was transferred to another ship of the auxiliary fleet, the USS *Alstede* (AF-46), a reefer, or refrigerated supply ship, aboard which I served out the remaining three months of my enlistment. I seem to have preserved nothing of the *Alstede* except the recollection of her excellent cuisine and her cleanliness, for by now shore matters were diverting my attention. There were weekend trips to New York to attend wild parties at my brother's place (I thought of them as civilian re-orientation seminars). There was a girl in Boston I had visited once and was looking forward to visiting again (the Pittsburgh flame had guttered out). There was a new motorcycle on its kickstand in a parking lot just outside the main gate. And above all, there was a growing anticipation of picking up where I had left off as artist and writer at the end of that ill-fated summer two years earlier. I was willing to try in earnest now.

When the *Alstede*'s re-enlistment officer browbeat me with his cursory spiel about "re-up" cash bonuses and what a fine *career* storekeeper I'd make, I just laughed in his face. I was gettin' out, man! Who was he kidding?

The day I received my honorable discharge, I draped my seabag across the motorcycle seat and throttled my way out of the Norfolk traffic to make a fast run to Greensboro, where my parents had just moved (my father would cap his teaching career at the University of North Carolina). My plan was to ditch my navy gear and pick up some civvies, hobnob with the old folks for a couple of days, then make a beeline to Boston, where . . . where I'd let the future take care of itself.

The later ride northward under clear skies was a feast of pleasantness. My new bike, a single-cylinder BMW, was proving to be a sweet and steady tourer. With sunlight glinting off its chrome, the black lacquer gleaming, and the onrushing wind making the visor of my Navy Exchange helmet sing like an Aeolian harp, I seemed to be piloting an empyreal chariot. In a purist's freedom, I ticked off the miles toward the Hub. The interstates were new then, relatively empty of traffic, and every expansion joint in the roadway offered up a beneficent *ba-bump*. The handgrips, the pin-striped gas tank between my knees, the comfortable Schorsch Meier seat, the footpegs—everything touched me just right. At sixty miles per hour, the motorcycle handled as lightly as a feather; only at the rest stops did I come down to earth. And then I walked so nobly to the restrooms and the water fountains, ambling with a languorous lankiness, Brando-like, helmet tucked under my arm—I, the youthful god of the highway, momentarily summoned from heaven by thirst, by the need to pee.

Wheeling into Boston just before dark, I called the girl and told her I had arrived. A dorm dweller, she arranged for me to spend the night with friends of hers, an extended family of BU students (and fellow motorcyclists) who lived in a crash-pad off Central Square. I navigated the familiar streets to their lodging, where I was given a fraternal welcome for having biked such a long way. It was an amazing night; my body was still very much in motion, still aiming my buzzing craft along the concrete canals. I lay there, ears humming with phantom road noise, trying to fall asleep in the houseful of hospitable strangers, alternately worried about the security of the Beamer parked on the street below (but protectively camouflaged in the regiment of house machines) and what I would do first on Day One, which was tomorrow. In time, I was soothed by the tang of incense and marijuana that drifted through the beaded curtain of the mattress-islanded room. Later, when it was assumed that I had drifted off, a couple clinked through the curtain and began making love beside me with a breathless rearing and shuddering, oblivious to my presence, and when that was over, I think I finally fell asleep.

The next morning, I began looking for a place to live. On the recommendation of a friend of a friend of the girl's (over crullers and coffee on her way to class) I found a vacant fourth-floor walkup on the uncouth side of Beacon Hill, at the back of a dead-end alley bisected by a bridge over which MTA trains thundered. It was a one-room garret, perfect for my needs, and its rent plus deposit took only a small chunk of the wad of bills, my navy severance pay, I had thrust down in my boots for safekeeping. The rest of the day I just toured around town, inebriated by the *il fait beau* of the cloudless, energizing October afternoon. What could I not accomplish with such rainless good luck? Who could I not become, having put every hurdle of growing up—nursery school, kindergarten, elementary school, high school, college, military service— behind me?

There was the nagging reality of the reserve meetings I was required by law to attend. I wrote the local Naval Reserve Board, proclaiming future noninvolvement. I stated that I had turned conscientious objector, which was philosophically true; having devoted twenty-four months to the war machine, I deplored war all the more. Grudgingly, the Board accepted my view.

Antiwar protest in Boston was at the flash point, and I was overcome with guilt when I compared my easy, East Coast enlistment to that which other young Americans were enduring in Southeast Asia. I grieved for the three or four inductees I had known personally who never came back. Luck had a price tag; in my case, it would give me a mistaken identity for several years until the government-issue component of my civilian wardrobe (pea coat, chambray shirts with my name stencilled over the pockets, bell bottom dungarees) eventually wore out. When people assumed I had served in Vietnam, I was made painfully aware of the consequences. There were no hugs, no handshakes, no free drinks. To the few who questioned me, I told the truth, although later, like the combat vets, I got in the habit of saying nothing at all. The front-page pictures of body bags and the week's casualty toll in headlines were making psycho-social pariahs of all former military personnel. Silence seemed to be the best available healing option.

I outfitted my garret with thrift-store furnishings: a mattress and spring set, a table, side chairs, flatware, a foursome of Melmac plates and cups, a black-bottomed aluminum skillet, a spaghetti steamer. I wired up one overhead bulb in an inverted flower pot and another in a pie tin. I bought a mixing connector for the two-tap sink and rigged a shower enclosure above the bathtub. I installed new weatherstripping around the draft-rattling windows, cleaning them inside and out for what must have been the first time in twenty years. Scanning my neighbors' curbside throwaways, I found curtains, an electric fan, a broken easel, a vinyl recliner. My oddest retrieval was a watertight carrying case (for use on the motorcycle) that had housed a 120-volt electrical skin-stimulating weight-loss contraption. Lastly, I painted my walls white, so that the three dormer windows (on three exposures) provided maximum illumination. Already I was knee-deep in thoughts about art and what it would take to harness the first flickers of inspiration.

The garret was truly home as soon as I could sleep through the night without waking in a panic whenever the trains roared past. Talk about atomic bomb dreams! Mine were ground zero replays, building-shaking pandemoniums that invaded my sleep-state with the cognizance of instant incineration. I'd jerk upright in a stupor with a stunned "Oh, *shit!*" on my lips, so dismayed that the powers-that-be hadn't been able to keep the old planet together. What a cryin', goddamn shame! But as the noise of the train receded toward Charles Street Station and the calm of the moon and the streetlamp recaptured the windows, I'd regain my composure. Already, by day, I was giving the intrusion no mind. Train, what train? When it finally softened to a mere tattoo in the night, a rumble-strip on the roadway of my unconscious, I likened it to a sound of nature—a *basso profundo cum* whippoorwill, or something like that.

Then I set about being who I wanted to become. Self-employment beckoned stronger than it ever had before. No one in my family, no one among my friends or acquaintances had made the leap successfully, *but this was absolutely what I wanted to do.* I wanted to take the solo risk.

This was my chance to become an artist. Ever since childhood I had had an inkling that I would be spending my life this way: producing art and living minimally off the proceeds. Now was the time to get started. I could paint, I could write, and I could better myself as I went along. I wasn't trying to get rich. I had enough money in my boots to tide me over for a few months. Having served a navy hitch, I was also entitled to unemployment benefits, if I didn't mind waiting in line once a week in the basement of a government building downtown.

Hell no, I didn't mind. I knew I was starting at the bottom, with not even one foot on the first rung. The biggest factor in my favor was a fool's optimism (the day would come, uh huh, the day would come). I rather relished being a nobody because the chances I could take were infinitely more interesting than the chances I couldn't. My future would require a long ladder to reach, and I'd have to be fearless once I got off the ground. Relentlessly, I encouraged myself to succeed.

I developed an unusual perspective: seeing myself in the mirror of my imagination. I saw what I looked like, who I had become – a young man in his mid-twenties, hale and happy, unattached but romantically inclined, saturated to the fingertips with talent. A young man who owned a vehicle that could get him anywhere and was easy to park. A young man whose grooming was abominable, but whose inner landscape was shipshape. A young man who was innocent and worldly in the same breath, a young man who had seen just enough of life to realize that his gas gauge of experience was hovering slightly above empty.

It is this person I have tried to preserve, this reborn civilian who motorcycled around greater Boston, keeping his finger on the pulse of his own humanity, watching sunrises and strip-teases, painting and writing, loving and losing, singing and being sung to. A rainbow of a person he was, complexly colored by every new sensation. He vanishes when I see the wrinkles on my face, when I ruminate upon the conical heap of sawdust that my years have piled. Oh, the gas gauge reads full now. There's paint and prose enough to encircle the earth twice over. There are moments when the earth shakes and even stops, when wonders appear before my eyes, when gratification – poetic, gustatory, sensual – blows me away. And I am wiser, I do not doubt. Yet I was at my best then, in Boston as the 1960s drew to a close. Cordoning off the prevailing avenues one by one, I had no future but the long shot of artistic recognition. I invested the better portion of my boot money in acrylic paint and canvas, in ream after ream of typing paper. I knew only that it would feel good to be busy again.

About the Author

Peter Svenson was born in 1944. He has a B.A. from Tufts University and an M.F.A. in painting from the University of North Carolina. His first book, *Battlefield: Farming a Civil War Battleground*, was nominated for a National Book Award for 1993. He lives in Cross Keys, Virginia.